THE
EATER
GUIDE TO
New York City

By the editors of Eater

Illustrations by Naomi Otsu

Abrams Image, New York

CONTENTS

Introduction 4

Chapter 1:
DOWNTOWN WEST
Dining 10
Shopping 17

A Brief History of
Dining in NYC 20

Late-Night Food 28

Chapter 2:
DOWNTOWN EAST
Dining 34
Shopping 41

NYC Essentials 46

Splurges 62

Spotlight: Staten Island 63

Chapter 3:
MIDTOWN & FLATIRON
Dining 68
Shopping 74

NYC Food Glossary 77

Chapter 4:
UPTOWN
Dining 84
Shopping 90

Bodegas 101 92

Spotlight: The Bronx 98

Chapter 5:
QUEENS
Dining 104
Shopping 110

A Perfect Twenty-Four
Hours (and Then Some)
in NYC 113

NYC Food Calendar 122

Chapter 6:
NORTH BROOKLYN
Dining 128
Shopping 134

Three New Yorker–
Approved
Overnight Trips 138

Breakfast and Brunch 146

Chapter 7:
THE REST OF BROOKLYN
Dining   **152**
Shopping   **158**

How to Get a Seat at the
Table: From Reservations
to Walk-Ins   162

Hotels with the
Best Food Built In   164

Where to Eat Near Major
Tourist Attractions   166

Acknowledgments   168
Contributors   169
Index   170

INTRODUCTION

What set Eater apart when it launched back in 2005 was not its coverage of food but its obsession with New York restaurants. Founding editors Ben Leventhal and Lockhart Steele covered restaurants as living, breathing entities that, like us humans, traversed milestones of buzzy and heady early days, steady midlife, and (more often than not) tragic deaths. They covered what was on the plate, but also went deep on the players behind the scenes, the music, vibe, clientele, and meaning restaurants held in their community.

That obsession with the restaurant as a whole life-form—existing in a broader ecosystem—has only deepened over the decades at Eater. We tell you about the history of the restaurants and the traditions behind them. We explore the meaning of restaurants as community hubs. We chronicle how restaurants transform neighborhoods and entire cities in real time. We tell you where to eat but also why it matters. And everything that Eater is today—more than twenty city sites, coverage of national and global dining trends, a television show, multiple video series, a cookbook, and now this guidebook—is born out of our original dedication to the most exciting food city in the world.

New York was the fitting birthplace for Eater as a food publication because it had, and still has, such a vibrant and dynamic, ever-changing restaurant landscape, making it easy to fuel the site's earliest days incessantly chronicling the scene's ups and downs.

Because there is no place that compares to New York when it comes to restaurants. This is a city where you can find, on the same block, Southeast Asian pastries, Ukrainian pierogi, and Danish pour-over coffee. It's a city where a subway ride can get you just about any type of cuisine your heart desires. It is a city where you have a bounty of options for food delivery at one in the morning. It is a city where you could ask one hundred people to suggest the best place to eat right now, and get one hundred different—and equally excellent—answers.

New Yorkers will say that you can never get bored of dining in the city. Whether they're drawn to the same local haunts or dedicate themselves to tracking restaurant openings and Instagram pop-ups, food lovers here tend to let their palates guide the way, pushing their comfort zones and geographic boundaries. And, for some reason, we're always willing to stand in endless lines.

To tackle it all, we split this massive city into seven large sections—mostly to help with planning and so that you're not spending all day in transit. Within each broad section, like Downtown West and North Brooklyn, Eater-approved restaurants and shops are organized alphabetically and were chosen based on how well they've stood the test of time, with a mix of New York icons and newer places that have fundamentally changed the dining scene in some way. The places here cover myriad cuisines and price points, vibes, and occasions.

We also dive into the history of dining in this town, the words you need to know, tips and tricks, and the context behind the real dining trends and dishes that you can get here and only here. We've included an hour-by-hour guide to our favorite food spots spanning multiple boroughs, a bodega primer, and, if you really must leave the city, highly recommended day trips. It was written by a whole team of Eater restaurant obsessives, who spend their days and nights studying the restaurant scene like London cabbies study the roads.

The idea of carrying a physical travel guide around might seem a bit antiquated. The phone in your pocket has some version of everything here and more, but information overload and decision fatigue are very real. With this guide, we aimed to distill years of insight and knowledge about New York to bring you a mix of our always reliable favorites and of-the-moment recommendations, in a travel-friendly format. Use this as a quick resource or a deep read on the subway as you bop from Midtown to Flushing and back again. We hope you take notes, dog-ear the pages, and circle your favorites. And if you're looking for the latest guidance from our editors, our QR codes will lead you to a bevy of updated maps and guides on the Eater site, where you can go as far down the rabbit hole as your heart, or stomach, can handle. The thing about New York is, you can barely fit all the eating you'd like to do into one lifetime—much less one visit. But, with our help, you sure can try.

— **Amanda Kludt**, publisher, and
Stephanie Wu, editor in chief

Chelsea
Greenwich Village
Meatpacking District
Soho
Tribeca
West Village

DOWN

1

TOWN
WEST

DOWNTOWN WEST

DINING

1. Altro Paradiso
2. Barbuto
3. Carbone
4. Charlie Bird
5. Cookshop
6. Corner Bistro
7. Dame
8. Ear Inn
9. El Quijote
10. Fanelli Cafe
11. Frenchette
12. Hector's Cafe & Diner
13. Jeffrey's Grocery
14. John's of Bleecker Street
15. King
16. Los Tacos No. 1 at Chelsea Market
17. Mamoun's Falafel
18. Minetta Tavern
19. NY Dosas
20. The Odeon
21. Raoul's
22. Semma
23. Shukette
24. Sullivan Street Bakery
25. Taïm
26. Txikito
27. Via Carota

SHOPPING

1. Chambers Street Wines
2. Chelsea Market
3. McNulty's Tea & Coffee Co.
4. Murray's Cheese
5. NY Cake
6. Porto Rico Importing Co.
7. Roman and Williams Guild
8. Tea & Sympathy
9. Té Company

Hudson River

Tribeca

WEST ST.

WORTH ST.

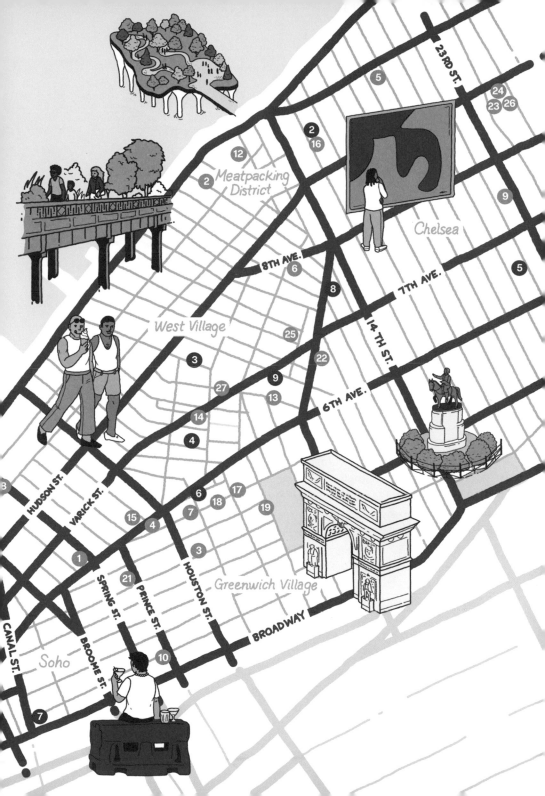

DOWNTOWN WEST
DINING

The west side of downtown Manhattan, which includes the neighborhoods of Tribeca, Soho, the West Village, Greenwich Village, and Chelsea, is a treasure trove for restaurant lovers and includes some of the buzziest spots with the hardest-to-get reservations.

The area was historically an enclave for some of our most famous artists—Bob Dylan in the West Village; Jimi Hendrix and William S. Burroughs in Greenwich Village; Patti Smith, Andy Warhol, and Iggy Pop at the Chelsea Hotel; and Jean-Michel Basquiat, Donald Judd, and Twyla Tharp in Soho's lofts. It still is, only now they're the kinds of artists who win Oscars and command many millions of dollars per project and can afford to live here.

Luckily, the restaurant scene is vibrant and varied, with options for every budget and cuisine preference.

Starting south in Tribeca, you'll find a mostly quiet residential neighborhood. It was once an industrial area that was taken over by artists in the seventies and eighties before becoming a refuge for the wealthy—who turned those artist lofts into giant condos—in the nineties, and still consistently ranks among Manhattan's most expensive neighborhoods. Tribeca does not have as dynamic a restaurant scene as neighborhoods to the north, but it boasts some destination-worthy food and local favorites.

Moving north, Soho is a shopping district that's packed with tourists and the requisite expensive-but-mediocre restaurants that cater to them. But a little digging reveals some real classics with notable followings.

Greenwich Village and the area around Washington Square Park still retains some of its bohemian charm and eclectic appeal, only now mixed in with bars, fast-casual joints, and cafés designed for the NYU crowd.

Meanwhile, the West Village is one of the city's loveliest neighborhoods, composed of stately brownstones dating from the 1800s, modest small storefronts with unique merchandise, and industrial architecture. This neighborhood was called "Little Bohemia" in the early 1900s due to its off-Broadway theaters, was home to the Beat movement in the fifties, and became a hotbed for social justice protests, including the Stonewall riots, a major catalyst for the LGBTQIA+ movement. In the nineties, it starred in *Sex and the City*, and continues to be home to some of the city's best people-watching.

Just above the West Village is the nightlife center of the Meatpacking District, which once housed the city's slaughterhouses and is now home to clubs, restaurants, designer retail, the Whitney Museum, and the start of the High Line, a greenway built over an old elevated rail line.

Take that High Line walkway up through Chelsea, also once an industrial neighborhood now known for its impressive array of art galleries and beautiful town houses. It's filled with small neighborhood spots that do brisk business on weekend afternoons, when visitors crowd the nearby galleries.

Not surprisingly, there's a wide variety of food to be had throughout this chunk of the city, but it's crowded, so plan ahead (see page 162 for tips on snagging a hot table). And note that for our purposes, we're including anything west of Broadway from the southern tip of the island up to Eighth Street and anything west of Fifth Avenue from Eighth Street to Thirtieth Street in this section. For anything east, see page 30.

1. Altro Paradiso
234 Spring Street,
Soho

After you burn some calories shopping in Soho, Altro Paradiso is a subdued-but-fancy way to treat yourself with some Roman classics. The restaurant is owned by Ignacio Mattos, behind Estela (page 36) and the food and beverage program at the Nine Orchard hotel (page 164). The menu often changes with each visit, but Altro Paradiso's cacio e pepe, made with a single, thick noodle that curls up on the plate, is a crowd favorite.

2. Barbuto
113 Horatio Street,
West Village

Yes, there is a wrong way to order at Barbuto. And it's by skipping the iconic chicken dish: crispy-skinned with salsa verde (shown below). Chef Jonathan Waxman's signature dish is beloved by locals and visitors alike.

3. Carbone
181 Thompson Street,
Greenwich Village

Consistently one of the most coveted reservations in town, Carbone is part theater, part nostalgia play, and all-around glamorous red-sauce restaurant. Behemoth, eye-poppingly expensive portions of dishes like their iconic spicy vodka sauce rigatoni and veal parm come served on a cart by waiters wearing designer uniforms in a swanky-but-fun dining room.

4. Charlie Bird
5 King Street,
Soho

A perennially popular spot, Charlie Bird serves up lighter pastas, like cavatelli with sausage, saffron, and mint. Don't miss the raw bar selection, which might include razor clams with fennel in addition to oysters and trout belly.

Among small plates, the seasonally changing farro is a highlight. Large plates are primarily seafood- and fowl-centric, and the wine selection makes this a hospitality industry hang, accompanied by a hip-hop soundtrack.

5. Cookshop
156 10th Avenue,
Chelsea

Cookshop was founded with a farm-to-table ethos in 2005 and has gradually grown to be a favorite spot for a tumultuous brunch or a quieter dinner in Chelsea. Vegetables are emphasized—even in its inventive pizzas—and there's a substantial commitment to seafood, while many appetizers and entrees are prepared in a wood-fired oven.

6. Corner Bistro
331 West 4th Street,
West Village

After walking the High Line or checking out the Whitney Museum, stop by this New York institution—a bar from 1961 that's famous for its burger. It's an affordable option, in a divey environment, that always makes for a truly New York experience.

7. Dame

87 MacDougal Street,
Greenwich Village

While English food doesn't always get the best rap here in the States, Dame is establishing a new high bar for the cuisine. Yes, the expertly prepared fish and chips made them famous when Dame was a pandemic pop-up, but this high-end, intensely hyped restaurant highlights all kinds of seafood dishes with a British twist, from crudos to squid skewers, grilled oysters, and whitefish croquettes. It's tiny and popular, so make a reservation in advance.

8. Ear Inn

326 Spring Street,
Soho

On the western fringes of Soho, this cozy pub is one of the oldest operating bars in NYC—it turned two hundred in 2017. A solid menu of pub fare includes a popular burger, mac and cheese, plus occasional surprises, like confit duck legs or smoked rainbow trout. All sorts of nautical ephemera line the walls.

9. El Quijote

226 West 23rd Street,
Chelsea

The Hotel Chelsea is a New York icon, a home to artists over the years, and though its history has been somewhat papered over by new construction, the lobby restaurant is as charming as ever. El Quijote first opened in 1930 and operated for decades before closing and relaunching in 2022, under the same team that owns popular Williamsburg restaurant Sunday in Brooklyn. The Spanish food here is great, but the ornate interior design is what makes it unlike any other in the city.

10. Fanelli Cafe

94 Prince Street,
Soho

A visit to Fanelli's is a step back in time, and no place in Soho evokes the nineteenth century and the area's cast-iron era more effectively. Over the years, Fanelli's has become popular with a younger, more fashionable crowd, making it a place to see and be seen. That doesn't mean the food here—bar fare like burgers and chili—isn't worth your time, but people-watching is prime.

It gets especially crowded on weekends and during happy hour, so plan accordingly.

11. Frenchette

241 West Broadway,
Tribeca

This high-end French brasserie from Lee Hanson and Riad Nasr, two alums of Balthazar (the iconic locale on page 35), caused a sensation when it opened in Tribeca in Spring 2018. Now working on their own terms, the duo looks to put modern spins on the French classics. There are dishes like duck frites, lobster beignets, and calf's head with gribiche—dishes rooted in old-school techniques without feeling stuffy. The team also has a nearby bakery that shares a name.

12. Hector's Cafe & Diner

44 Little West 12th Street,
Meatpacking District

Opened in 1949, Hector's is one of the last remaining vestiges of the Meatpacking District, a place where meatcutters and haulers would hang out after deliveries or before work at four or five A.M. It is in many ways a conventional diner, though the menu is built out with Mexican dishes—and for a diner, the food is above average. It's a fun and inexpensive place to eat after exploring the Meatpacking District.

13. Jeffrey's Grocery
172 Waverly Place,
West Village

A neighborhood spot, beloved for its oysters and other seafood specialties, this restaurant is owned by Happy Cooking, a hospitality group with a number of West Village heavy hitters. Most of the menu has a salty, oceanic twist, like deviled eggs with furikake, or a Caesar salad with bagel chips and bonito flakes—ideal on a sticky summer day when you'd rather be by the shore.

14. John's of Bleecker Street
278 Bleecker Street,
West Village

One of NYC's oldest pizza parlors, open since 1929, comes from owner John Sasso, an alum of pizza icon Lombardi's (page 51). Eater NY critic Robert Sietsema calls it one of the best pies in the city. Baked in coal ovens, the pizza comes with toppings like ricotta or sliced meatballs. No slices are sold here, so come ready to order a full pie.

15. King
18 King Street,
Soho

Clare de Boer and Jess Shadbolt opened this elegant, tranquil West Village restaurant in 2016, bringing experience from London's acclaimed River Café. Regally plated dishes here change nightly, but expect seasonally driven options like trout, zucchini, saffron rice, and sorbets in flavors like hyssop or quince. The chefs also have an Italian restaurant, Jupiter, in Rockefeller Center.

16. Los Tacos No. 1 at Chelsea Market
75 9th Avenue,
Chelsea

Since opening at the market back in 2013, Los Tacos' lines have been largely unwavering, and the restaurant has since spawned several outposts throughout the city, including in Times Square. Despite now being more of a chain, they still serve some of the city's best tacos. Los Tacos No. 1 also has an adjoining, destination-worthy Mexican seafood spot called Los Mariscos, and serves breakfast burritos in the morning.

17. Mamoun's Falafel
119 MacDougal Street,
Greenwich Village

A favorite among NYU students and nearby Comedy Cellar attendees, Mamoun's is universally beloved for its affordable falafel sandwiches, which have been served in Greenwich Village since 1971. It's a casual, tiny to-go spot that stays open late. Lines will form, but they move fast.

18. Minetta Tavern
113 MacDougal Street,
Greenwich Village

Restaurateur Keith McNally (also behind Balthazar, page 35, and Pastis) is an expert in maintaining downtown Manhattan restaurants that stand the test of time—and in this case he breathed new life into a dusty Greenwich Village classic, transforming a red-sauce joint into a destination steak house. Come for all things beef: steak frites, roasted bone marrow, and of course, its iconic Black Label burger, served with caramelized onions. Prices run high, but it's an experience nonetheless, even if you're just stopping by for a drink.

19. NY Dosas
50 Washington Square South,
Greenwich Village

This food truck located in Washington Square Park is a go-to for students and other New Yorkers looking for a portable, low-priced lunch that's also vegetarian-friendly. Thiru Kumar, aka the Dosa Man, is famous across the city for these crispy, crunchy savory pancakes, made daily and filled with various vegetables and potatoes. Lines run long, but it's worth the wait.

20. The Odeon

145 West Broadway,
Tribeca

When the Odeon opened in 1980, it was a Tribeca spot that was as much about seeing and being seen as it was about the food. The party restaurant quickly became a downtown icon among the fashion set especially, referenced in everything from Jay McInerney's *Bright Lights, Big City* to the *Saturday Night Live* opening credits. These days, it's a perfect place to pull up for a martini and a shrimp cocktail.

21. Raoul's

180 Prince Street,
Soho

The draw at this longtime French bistro has been the burger, even though it was only available semi-secretly in limited supply at the bar. But now it's been added to the regular brunch menu, composed of a pepper-corn-crusted brisket blend, seared in butter, topped with creamy Saint-André cheese, watercress, onions, and cornichons, and served on a challah bun with duck-fat fries and cream-and-cognac sauce. Beyond the burger, opt for bistro classics like escargot, pâté, frisée with lardons and a poached egg, or steak au poivre. They also own modern luncheonette Revelie across the street.

22. Semma

60 Greenwich Avenue,
West Village

From the team behind Dhamaka (page 36), Semma is a splurge-worthy West Village option showcasing South Indian specialties rarely, if ever, seen in the city: There's the triangular gunpowder dosa, snails served in a banana leaf package, and spicy lamb sukka. Call in advance to preorder the Dungeness crab dish—there are only a few available per night—which arrives so saucy they give you a bib.

23. Shukette

230 9th Avenue,
Chelsea

After gallery hopping or a stroll on the High Line, Shukette is one of the coolest restaurants in the area to make a stop. Ayesha Nurdjaja's follow-up to her West Village restaurant Shuka is even better than its sibling, known for its vegetable-forward menu and extensive "rip and dip" section, as well as its can't-skip tahini soft serve.

24. Sullivan Street Bakery

236 9th Avenue,
Chelsea

A branch of the prized bakery that opened in Soho in 1994, this handsome and trim lunchroom serves pastries and egg breakfasts in the mornings before switching to sandwiches and Roman pizzas until closing. The custard-squirting bomboloni, either vanilla or chocolate, are worth seeking out, as are the loaves of bread and square slices of focaccia topped with ingredients like potatoes and zucchini, available all day.

25. Taïm

222 Waverly Place,
West Village

This tiny West Village store-front first opened in 2005 and has since spawned several outposts in NYC and beyond. All serve reliable, affordable Middle Eastern food, but this location deserves special attention simply because it offers an affordable lunch or dinner in a neighborhood that's increasingly pricey. Falafel comes either as a pita sand-wich (shown above) or as a bowl with bases of hummus, rice, couscous, or greens. Seating is extremely limited, so it's best eaten to-go in Washington Square Park or crashing on a nearby stoop.

QR CODES
for our online
guides to
DOWNTOWN WEST
neighborhoods:

CHELSEA

SOHO

TRIBECA

WEST VILLAGE

26. Txikito

240 9th Avenue,
Chelsea

Txikito's highlights include Basque small plates of octopus, poached cod, beef cheek and jowl, and king oyster mushroom carpaccio. The chefs are the wife-and-husband team of Alex Raij and Eder Montero, and the premises recalls a Spanish tapas bar in its style and intimacy.

27. Via Carota

51 Grove Street,
West Village

Via Carota—owned by the duo behind nearby French hot spot Buvette, lasagna icon I Sodi, and the Shaker-inspired Commerce Inn— may be a perfect restaurant. Even the simplest green salad is a revelation here, but do not miss the tagliatelle with prosciutto and peas (shown above), the artichokes with parm, or the risotto with Meyer lemon. If you can't get a reservation, go early, stick to small parties, and plan to wait. Note the team also owns Bar Pisellino across the street, a perfect spot for Italian spritzes and other snacks to help with your wait.

DOWNTOWN WEST
SHOPPING

From art gallery–rich Chelsea down to the cobblestoned streets of Tribeca, an appreciation of food and dining carries through many retail destinations in this part of town. Start at Chelsea Market and make your way south to the winding, Paris-like streets of the West Village, where coffee and tea shops that have been around long enough to have fueled the Beat Generation have become neighborhood institutions. While in Soho, visit the food lover's version of the high-fashion boutiques that court international shoppers and New Yorkers alike.

1. Chambers Street Wines

148 Chambers Street,
Tribeca

Chambers Street Wines is one of the best wine shops in the city, if not the country. Since 2001, well ahead of the current fanaticism for the genre, the shop has specialized in natural wines, particularly those from small producers in the Loire Valley, Champagne, Burgundy, the Rhone, Piedmont, and Germany. Aside from its vast selection, the Tribeca shop is known for its conversational approach to service, which almost guarantees your leaving with a bottle you'll love.

2. Chelsea Market

75 9th Avenue,
Chelsea

Located inside a former factory building in the Meatpacking District, Chelsea Market is one of those spaces that's shared by both visitors and New York natives. It was once thought of as a tourist trap, but the recent addition of quality restaurants like Los Mariscos and Los Tacos No. 1 (page 14) has renewed the interest of local food lovers and nearby office workers. After lunch, stop by the stalls for halva brand Seed + Mill; cheese shop Saxelby Cheesemongers; Li-Lac Chocolates, which bills itself as Manhattan's oldest chocolate maker; and an outpost of Pearl River Mart, a longtime purveyor of Asian-inspired goods, including snacks, tableware, and cooking tools.

3. McNulty's Tea & Coffee Co.

109 Christopher Street,
West Village

McNulty's is one of those New York City shops that feels of another time. You'll see some familiar boxed tea brands on shelves along the walls, but the vast majority of the limited space is overtaken by jars filled with loose-leaf tea. Vintage weighing equipment behind the counter adds to the apothecary-like feel. But there's no need to be intimidated, as McNulty's tea blends are also available in convenient canisters that come with helpful descriptions of their contents.

4. Murray's Cheese

254 Bleecker Street,
West Village

Situated on perpetually bustling Bleecker Street, the Murray's flagship store has everything you need to put together the cheese board of your dreams (wood and slate boards included) and a staff ready to point you in the right direction. No one would fault you for spending some time poking around—while real estate is often scant in downtown New York City shops, Murray's airy space offers plenty of room to browse, plus a room upstairs where it holds cheese classes.

5. NY Cake

118 West 22nd Street,
Chelsea

NY Cake is a veritable warehouse of baking supplies, stocking literally hundreds of sprinkles, cookie cutters, silicone molds, and just about anything else you could possibly need to take on a baking project (minus the perishable ingredients). In 2018, the longtime store moved from just down the street to this much-bigger location, and it's taken advantage of the additional space with a dedicated area for baking classes and private events and workshops.

6. Porto Rico Importing Co.

201 Bleecker Street, Greenwich Village

A longtime Village institution, since 1907, Porto Rico sells beans for brewing from around the world, on display in bulk burlap bags. You can also grab a cup for the road. And while the aroma of coffee may overwhelm the senses, note that Porto Rico also sells hundreds of varieties of loose-leaf tea.

7. Roman and Williams Guild

53 Howard Street, Soho

For the person who wants to populate their home with elegant objets d'art, there's Roman and Williams Guild. Dinnerware and glassware collections come from expert artisans—and the prices underscore this point. The shop flows seamlessly into La Mercerie, an appropriately chic French restaurant and café led by chef Marie-Aude Rose. There, you can try out some of the Roman and Williams Guild wares, even if you can't justify the splurge to take them home.

8. Tea & Sympathy

108 Greenwich Avenue, West Village

Situated immediately next door to the British comfort food restaurant of the same name, Tea & Sympathy stocks everything a home-sick Brit could hope for, from Cadbury chocolate to Walkers crisps, plus tea and all the requisite accessories. Nearby, Myers of Keswick is another great option for pork pies, sausage rolls, and more if you want to make it a proper crawl.

9. Té Company

163 West 10th Street, West Village

On a quiet block of the West Village, up the stairs of what would at first glance seem to be a purely residential building, Té Company is a Taiwanese teahouse first. For tea enthusiasts, the tiny shop at the entrance is also worth a visit for the loose-leaf tea—including two dozen varieties of oolong—and expert-level brewing

supplies. Tea snacks are for sale, and the shop's beloved pineapple linzer cookies are sure to please anyone, regardless of their stance on tea.

BEYOND RESTAURANTS

Coffee Shops
Café Kitsune
Do Not Feed Alligators
Felix Roasting Co.
Hungry Ghost
Joe Coffee Company
Oslo Coffee Roasters

Bars
Bandits
Bar Pisellino
Dante
Donna
The Happiest Hour
Katana Kitten
Milady's
The Raines Law Room

Bakeries
ALF Bakery
Fabrique Bakery
Frenchette Bakery
Grandaisy Bakery
Mah-Ze-Dahr
Patisserie Fouet

Ice Cream
Mochidoki
Morgenstern's Finest Ice Cream

A BRIEF HISTORY OF DINING IN NYC

By Robert Sietsema

When the *Half Moon*—the Dutch ship commanded by Henry Hudson—appeared on the eastern horizon in 1609, the Canarsee tribe may have been gathered around a fire pit on the shore of Flushing Bay. They were one of several Indigenous groups who inhabited the area now known as New York City. Their pit might have been lined with clams, which they plucked out and ate, savoring their juiciness and smokiness, later recycling the shells for a variety of purposes, including wampum, a form of money used between the Native Americans and the Dutch.

When the Dutch arrived, the locals were agricultural people with staples like corn, squash, and beans, who hunted for deer, elk, wild turkey, and small game. They were fond of soups, corn bread, and salads—a contrast, especially by modern nutritional standards, to the bread, bread, and more bread, sometimes with cheese, that the Dutch and, forty years later, the English colonists ate. Beyond the bread and cheese, one of the most delicious culinary contributions of the Dutch, however, is probably donuts, which were often sold on the streets in open-air markets. Indeed, fried dough in all its forms became a durable leitmotif of NYC's food, as seen in today's Italian street-fair zeppoles, the Mexican churros sold from trays in subway stations, and the youtiao often served with congee in Chinatown.

For its first three centuries, New York remained an agricultural hub. As the city expanded outward from its original Lower Manhattan settlement, wild berries remained at the margins, and farmers grew grains like corn, wheat, rice, barley, and oats, as well as crops inherited from the Native Americans like squash and beans in what we now call Brooklyn and Queens, with farms organized into small communities that acted as trading centers. Fruit trees were also cultivated, varying the diet of the new republic beyond bread, cheese, meat pies, and beer. The Dutch presence can still be felt all over the five boroughs in well-preserved farmhouses (like Upper Manhattan's Dyckman Farmhouse) and in place names like Van Cortlandt Park in the Bronx and Brooklyn's Schermerhorn Street.

Not surprisingly, New York's waters were key to feeding the new city. They teemed with seafood of all sorts, including clams, oysters, and lobsters, all of which could be harvested just offshore, often without a boat. In colonial times, lobsters were so abundant they were often fed to prisoners. And bigger, too: legend has it a four-hundred-pound specimen washed ashore in the Battery during an eighteenth-century hurricane.

The famously polluted Gowanus Canal, located in one of Brooklyn's trendiest neighborhoods, was once a creek called "Gowanes" that became one of the most productive shellfish gathering spots. Though at first primarily clams were harvested there, oysters gradually began to exceed them in popularity, partly because they could most readily be enjoyed raw. In addition, the enhanced transportation systems of the mid-nineteenth century meant that fresh oysters could be whisked rapidly to Manhattan, not only from the Gowanus Canal and Sheepshead

Bay, but from points farther out on Long Island. (Now conservationists are actually using oysters and other bivalves to try to filter toxins from waterways surrounding the city.)

Before Manhattan was awash in hot dogs and pizza, raw oysters were the predominant form of fast food. Grand palaces of oysterdom dotted downtown by 1850, the most famous of which, Downing's Oyster House, was founded in 1825 at the corner of Broad and Wall Streets and operated until 1871. Thomas Downing, a freed slave who was also a prominent abolitionist, personally picked all the oysters that were served in his establishment. "Oyster cellars," or "oyster bars," followed—usually down a flight of stairs, at a bar that served shots and beer while oysters were continuously shucked and offered at all-you-can-eat prices of ten cents or so. Apparently, if you stayed too long and abused the privilege, you were purposefully served a bad oyster.

The last oyster bed in New York was shut down in 1927 due to pollution and overfishing. While oysters are still a prevalent dish at both upscale restaurants and neighborhood bar happy hours—and even include oysters from nearby Long Island—they aren't the street food they were one hundred years ago.

In 1827, Italian-Swiss brothers Giovanni and Pietro Delmonico opened what was first a pastry shop on William Street. Eventually, in the French style, set meals were added, and an empire grew over the next two centuries. One last branch remains on Beaver Street, said to be decorated with original columns from Pompeii. Delmonico's wasn't just the most expensive New York restaurant in the early nineteenth century; it was almost the only one. An evolution of the table d'hôte institutions of France, where a single set meal of many courses was provided at a fixed price, Delmonico's offered a bewildering number of choices for each course, many involving fish or game (like turtle soup and bear steaks), with options for French, English, or German recipes.

As the nineteenth century drew to a close, plenty of restaurants offered steaks and chops, serving a well-off social class that was still decidedly below Delmonico's customer base. Main courses of goose, mutton chops, chicken pot-pies, ham and eggs, or tripe might be served with a starter of soup and dessert of apple pudding. Keens Steakhouse, founded in 1885 in Midtown and formerly called Keens Chophouse, is a prime example; the mutton chop's still on the menu (see page 71).

So, if not in restaurants, where were most nineteenth-century New Yorkers eating? Men often ate beef stew or corned beef and cabbage in taverns, which had more limited food options and mostly catered to drinkers. Drugstores and other shops sometimes included simple lunch counters—later, these became stand-alone institutions. And the earliest diners were inspired by dining cars from railroad trains, prefabricated and then parked at street corners and in vacant lots starting in the late 1800s. In 1912, a sort of diner off-shoot opened in Times Square: the Automat. This unique self-service establishment displayed dishes in windowed nooks, to be purchased with coins and carried to your table. The Automat might be gone, but its spirit lives on in fast-casual joints like Sweetgreen and Pret A Manger, its direct descendants.

The arrival of non-European immigrants, beginning in the nineteenth century but accelerating in the twentieth, created a marvelous melting pot of international cuisines that has come to define food in the city, with fusion and innovation a controlling principle.

Another commonality of these early eateries, including the oyster cellar, the diner, and the lunch counter, was that meals were eaten rapidly—today's idea of relaxing while enjoying a meal was virtually nonexistent among the lower social classes, who did not have the time, money, or inclination to eat at a fancy restaurant or chophouse. You ate what you could find and ran. Early lunch counters, for example, would give you no more than twenty minutes to eat, and then your stool had to be vacated for the next customer.

Street food was flourishing in New York City even before the Revolutionary War, and throughout the past 250 years, one could make a light meal of a massive, well-salted pretzel; handful of roasted chestnuts; donut or Viennese sweet roll; or steamed sausage—our most ancient and durable forms of street food. But throughout this period the majority of New Yorkers ate at home or in board-inghouses that provided meals at an extra charge. And many residents quite literally didn't know where their next meal was coming from, a truth that is sadly unchanged today.

New York's most famous fast food might be the hot dog, all beef with a skin made of sheep's intestine—hence the salty pop when you bite into them. They can still be bought from a type of cart invented in 1914 that you'll find in front of the Metropolitan Museum of Art, at every other turn in Central Park, and throughout Times Square. The hot dog as we know it originated in Coney Island in 1915, when Nathan's—an empire named for hot-dog hawker Nathan Handwerker—was founded. Its flagship is still there, and worth visiting at the terminus of a host of subway lines (page 155). You'll also find them at Gray's Papaya (page 86) on the Upper West Side and Fulton Hot Dog King in downtown Brooklyn, or at a Jewish deli like Katz's (page 36) or Liebman's (page 98). The conventional condiments are limited to sauerkraut, mustard, and a sweet onion relish, said to have been invented by Greek vendors.

But New York's most beloved food? That's pizza. Throughout much of the twentieth century, "two slices and a Coke" may have been the most popular workers' lunch, and the neighborhood pizzeria became the foremost staple of cheap dining. Though it was invented in Naples, Italy, the first big, shareable, opulently topped pizza was created here at Lombardi's in 1905. Before that, freshly baked focaccia ruled the many tiny Italian groceries and bakeries that dotted the Lower East Side, Little Italy, and Greenwich Village. The original pizzerias, like Lombardi's, John's of Bleecker Street (page 14), and Patsy's in East Harlem, all used coal ovens, which burn fiercely hot, but around 1950 the cooler, gas-burning, stacked pizza oven was invented, making possible small neighborhood pizzerias that reheated and sold slices, a hallmark of our pizza culture.

While European-inspired food dominated New York City restaurants for most of its early history, cuisines from other parts of the world ascended at the dawn of the twentieth century. Manhattan's Chinatown began to grow in earnest in the 1870s, when the neighborhood consisted of three streets—Mott, Pell, and Doyers—that remain its modern hub. Tea shops and small cafés served dumplings and over-rice dishes, mainly to a population of Chinese immigrants until tourists began to arrive, and larger, more formal restaurants—some featuring musicians and dancers—began to cater to them. The largest and grandest was Port Arthur Restaurant on Mott Street, founded in 1897, with a menu finely honed to the modern tastes in Chinese American food with dishes like chop suey, chow mein, pepper steak, and egg foo young. (It closed in 1959.)

Racist immigration laws like the Chinese Exclusion Act of 1882 kept Chinatown's population confined mainly to men until the Immigration and Nationality Act of 1965, but the neighborhood still gradually solidified, expanded, and became famous for its food, an amalgam of dishes from Guangzhou and Chaoshan, modified with American ingredients.

Increasingly, Chinese restaurants were patronized by non-Chinese, who'd fallen in love with this obviously non-European cuisine. You can still get a taste of old-fashioned Chinese American dishes at Hop Kee and Wo Hop on the oldest part of Mott Street, the latter dating to 1938.

Eventually, Chinese restaurants would be found in every borough, from predictable neighborhood spots to those serving specific regional cuisines from Hunan, Shanxi, Yunnan, or Fujian. Sichuan food has taken the city by storm in the past two decades, with its fiery stir-fries and hot pots, and has become in some ways the city's dominant Chinese cuisine. Today you can find some of the best Sichuan fare in locales that are not traditional Chinese neighborhoods, such as at Szechuan Mountain House in the East Village, or Little Pepper in College Point, Queens.

A Sri Lankan acrobat opened the city's first Indian restaurant, called Ceylon India Inn, near Times Square in 1913, but Jackson Heights, Queens, emerged as New York's premier Indian neighborhood in the 1970s. Jackson Diner (page 106) opened in 1980 in a former diner, popularizing dishes like the fermented-rice-and-lentil crepe known as the dosa and the snacky samosa, a tetrahedral potato-stuffed pie, both of which have become NYC staples.

Soon there were Indian temples, groceries, and restaurants in neighborhoods like Murray Hill, the East Village, and Flushing, and another across the river in Journal Square, Jersey City. In Jackson Heights, the Indian restaurants were joined by Pakistani, Nepalese, and Tibetan ones. Even the Upper West Side, a traditionally Puerto Rican and Jewish neighborhood, became a bastion of Indian restaurants. In the modern era, upscale Indian restaurants like Gupshup, Baar Baar, and Dhamaka (page 36) are wildly popular.

You can't talk about the history of dining in New York without talking about bodegas—so integral to the city's food history that an entire section of this book is dedicated to them (see page 92). Bodega means "cellar" in Spanish, and the earliest version of the corner groceries you see now popped up in Brooklyn in the early twentieth century, most often owned and operated by Puerto Rican immigrants. They're places to buy staples like cornmeal and canned beans, soft drinks and beer, but they're also places where New Yorkers make friends, get their packages delivered, and order some of the best sandwiches in the city, like the chopped cheese, served hot on a hero roll with ground beef, onions, and melted American cheese.

In the 1980s, many bodegas were run by Mexican immigrants from the state of Puebla, who often installed taquerias in the back and used the fresh chiles, cactus paddles, and imported white cheeses found in store, with tortillas from the nearby tortillerias springing up everywhere. Visit Bushwick's Tortilleria Mexicana Los Hermanos to try a taqueria inside a tortilleria. Soon we had a more elaborate series of Mexican eateries reflecting the cuisine from places as far-flung as Oaxaca, Mexico City, Jalisco, and Sonora.

Meanwhile, Venezuelan immigrants brought their arepas with them; Salvadorans their pupusas; Australians their meat pies and breads; Nigerians their fufus and pepper soups; and Ukrainians their borscht. Spaniards brought their paellas; Egyptians their fava bean fouls; Serbs and Croats their cevapi sausages; Trinidadians their rotis and doubles; and Jamaicans their jerk chicken. Pakistanis brought their haleem; Taiwanese their stinky tofu and fly's head (a facetiously named stir-fry of pork and garlic chives); Koreans their barbecued meats and fermented kimchis; Brazilians their moquecas and feijoadas. The Lebanese, Palestinians, Syrians, Israelis, and Egyptians brought the now ubiquitous falafel sandwich and shawarma over rice.

The city's come a long way since the Dutch with their bread and cheese. Suffice it to say New York City is the greatest showcase of the world's foodways at all price points. Enjoy!

LATE-NIGHT FOOD

It may be known as the city that never sleeps, but it's often hard to find a great restaurant when you need one after prime time. These spots have you covered.

Birria-Landia
Multiple locations

Birria-Landia (page 105), the Jackson Heights food truck that launched a wave of birria taco spots in NYC, stays open until one A.M. or later, depending on location.

Coppelia
207 West 14th Street, Chelsea, Manhattan

Coppelia, an unassuming twenty-four-hour luncheonette, leans Mexican and Cuban but also serves oxtail empanadas, lomo saltado, and other dishes that draw from the Caribbean and Central and South America.

Court Square Diner
45-30 23rd Street, Long Island City, Queens

Not much has changed at Court Square Diner since brothers Steve and Nick Kanellos started running the joint in 1991, even as Long Island City has welcomed glitzy food halls and developments to the neighborhood. The twenty-four-hour diner serves a standard, multi-page diner menu with Jell-O, fifteen different omelets, and hulking hero sandwiches.

Dim Sum Palace
27 Division Street, Chinatown, Manhattan

It's one of few places in Chinatown to stay open past midnight, but the food, including barbecue pork buns and roast duck spring rolls, would be good at any hour.

The Donut Pub
740 Broadway, Noho, Manhattan

The newer and glitzier location of longtime icon the Donut Pub is open twenty-four hours for those in need of a sugar rush in the wee hours.

Empanada Mama
Multiple locations

The Hell's Kitchen and Lower East Side outposts of this late-night favorite (page 69) serve Colombian fare twenty-four hours a day.

Girasol Bakery
690 5th Avenue, Park Slope, Brooklyn

This South Slope bakery with a cafeteria-like dining room churns out huaraches, cemitas, and other Mexican dishes twenty-four hours a day. There's a vending machine stocked with Takis, spicy Cheetos, and Flamin' Hot chips at the back of the space, and a pastry case lined with colorful pan dulce up front. From the grill, try the breakfast burrito, a unique version of the dish made with hunks of potato, scrambled egg, and American cheese.

Hadramout Restaurant
172 Atlantic Avenue, Cobble Hill, Brooklyn

Big portions of Yemeni cuisine are the calling card at this twenty-four-hour restaurant, sandwiched between Clinton and Court Streets on Atlantic Avenue's heavily Middle Eastern corridor.

Halal carts
Multiple locations

The city is dotted with halal carts serving chicken and gyro sandwiches into the wee hours. Our favorite is Sammy's, with twenty-four-hour locations in Jackson Heights and Greenwich Village.

Kang Ho Dong Baekjeong NYC
1 East 32nd Street, Koreatown, Manhattan

There are Korean barbecue spots that stay open later, but Baekjeong (page 71) is our favorite after-hours spot in the area because of its rowdy vibes and quality cuts of meat.

La Isla
1439 Myrtle Avenue, Bushwick, Brooklyn

Puerto Rican mainstay La Isla specializes in blood sausage, pig ear, pernil, and a handful of other pork-based snacks served twenty-four hours a day. The late-night lunch counter also boasts an impressive selection of juices, including tamarind and grape flavors.

Mamoun's Falafel
119 MacDougal Street,
Greenwich Village, Manhattan

Some five decades after opening in Greenwich Village, Mamoun's Falafel continues to serve one of the city's most iconic late-night meals, until three A.M. on Thursdays and four A.M. on Fridays and Saturdays.

Papaya Dog
333 6th Avenue, West Village, Manhattan

Papaya Dog is one of those brightly lit twenty-four-hour corner hot dog spots that used to be much more common.

Pocha 32
15 West 32nd Street, 2nd floor,
Koreatown, Manhattan

This Korean pub (page 72) serves wings, spicy Kimchi stews, and soju until late.

Sunny & Annie's
94 Avenue B, Alphabet City, Manhattan

The creativity of the options at this beloved 24/7 deli is unparalleled, with combinations like bulgogi and cantaloupe on a roll, and names often referencing pop culture or politics.

Superiority Burger
119 Avenue A, Alphabet City, Manhattan

The famous veggie burgers (page 38) can be found on the late-night menu, available until two A.M. from Thursday to Saturday, along with the incredible gelato and sorbet.

Alphabet City
Chinatown
East Village
Financial District
Gramercy Park
Little Italy
Lower East Side
Noho
Nolita
Union Square

DOWN

2

TOWN
EAST

DOWNTOWN EAST

DINING

1. B&H Dairy
2. Balthazar
3. Banh Mi Saigon
4. Bobwhite Counter
5. Cafe Mogador
6. Casa Adela
7. Cervo's
8. Cocoron
9. Dhamaka
10. El Castillo de Jagua
11. Estela
12. Factory Tamal
13. Golden Diner
14. Katz's Delicatessen
15. Kiki's
16. Kopitiam
17. Miss Lily's
18. Momofuku Noodle Bar
19. Nom Wah Tea Parlor
20. Punjabi Deli
21. Scarr's Pizza
22. Shu Jiao Fu Zhou
23. Spicy Village
24. Superiority Burger
25. Taiwan Pork Chop House
26. Thai Diner
27. The Tin Building
28. Uncle Lou
29. Veselka
30. Wildair
31. Wu's Wonton King
32. Yellow Rose
33. Yi Ji Shi Mo

SHOPPING

1. Bonnie Slotnick Cookbooks
2. Coming Soon
3. Despaña
4. Di Palo's Fine Foods
5. Economy Candy
6. Essex Market and Market Line
7. John Derian Company Inc.
8. The Meadow
9. Nalata Nalata
10. The Pickle Guys
11. Russ & Daughters
12. SOS Chefs
13. Stick With Me Sweets
14. Union Square Greenmarket
15. Wing On Wo & Co.
16. Yunhong Chopsticks

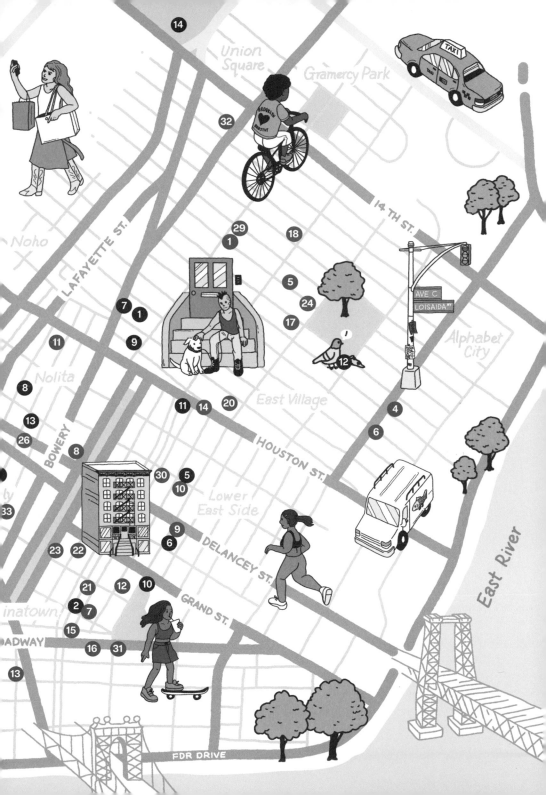

DOWNTOWN EAST
DINING

From the East Village to the Lower East Side, Chinatown, and Nolita, the east side of downtown New York stakes its claim as Manhattan's "coolest" neighborhood zone. Decades ago, the East Village was the home of the punk movement. In the 1970s, bands like Television, the Ramones, and the Velvet Underground all played at venues like the now-shuttered, legendary CBGB. Vestiges of the old St. Marks Place, a go-to area for buying vintage and records and getting piercings and tattoos, remain. But these days, the strip is more often frequented for its karaoke bars and fast-casual dining.

In the midst of a neighborhood holding on to its Ukrainian roots (Veselka the most famous among them), today's East Village isn't punk in its truest sense of the word, but it retains some of that youthful, DIY energy it was known for and is a favorite among college students from NYU, Cooper Union, and the New School. At the northern end, near Union Square, the Strand is still one of the city's most iconic—and biggest—bookstores. Farther east is Tompkins Square Park, lined with bars and restaurants, which doubles as a popular skater spot. It's become known as a place where up-and-coming creative chefs can make a name for themselves (as David Chang of Momofuku did back in the early 2000s).

The Lower East Side is similarly appealing to younger people looking to go out. At the turn of the twentieth century, the neighborhood below East Houston Street was known for its tenements crowded with immigrants from all over the world, and its vibrant Jewish community that opened various pickle stores and bagel shops—a breeding ground for foods now considered iconic. Today's Lower East Side is a lot different, but equally busy, with bars, hip restaurants, and a thriving fashion scene.

The number-one food neighborhood you can't miss is Manhattan's Chinatown. Here, you'll find plenty of regional Chinese restaurants, including Cantonese spots, dim sum parlors, carts selling translucent rice rolls, bubbling Sichuan food, and Taiwanese bubble tea, as well as Vietnamese food and even old-school red-sauce spots from overlapping Little Italy. Follow the main artery of Canal Street and turn down one of the many restaurant-filled side streets teeming with options. For those on a budget, Chinatown has a delightful, diverse array of incredibly affordable choices.

Finally we have Nolita, home to chic designer boutiques, trendy restaurants, and the fashion-forward crowds that frequent them and what's left of Little Italy, which has shrunk to a few tourist-laden blocks with a handful of old-school gems.

1. B&H Dairy
127 2nd Avenue,
East Village

Open since the 1930s, B&H Dairy's entirely kosher menu ranges from blintzes and matzo brei to tuna melts, pierogi, and more. Most dishes come with a complimentary side of buttered challah, there's free refills on coffee, and daily combo platters are an especially good deal. It's easy to feel stuffed with just $20 here.

2. Balthazar
80 Spring Street,
Nolita

Another McNally classic (see also page 14), Balthazar opened in 1997 and reimagined what a French brasserie could look, feel, and taste like stateside. It's been influential throughout its life and is still one of the best spots for a celebrity sighting. Wait times run long accordingly. Go for classics like French onion soup, and, of course, steak with crispy French fries (shown above). It has an adjoining bakery with baguettes and other pastries that are carried at coffee shops around the city.

3. Banh Mi Saigon
198 Grand Street,
Little Italy

It can be hard to find an affordable meal under $10 in Manhattan, but Banh Mi Saigon is a go-to. Banh mi are served with the expected shredded and pickled daikon and carrots, julienned cucumber, a sprig of cilantro, and fresh jalapeños, but the baguettes here are made in-house.

4. Bobwhite Counter
94 Loisaida Avenue,
Alphabet City

Considered to be one of the best spots in Manhattan to find fried chicken, Bobwhite offers sandwiches in buffalo, barbecue, or classic with bread-and-butter pickles. The sleeper hit is the fried chicken Caesar salad wrap. Be sure to get the pimento dip on the side.

5. Cafe Mogador
101 St. Marks Place,
East Village

This low-key brunch spot opened in 1983 and is still a go-to among local regulars. Favorites here include the Moroccan-style poached eggs served in a spicy tomato stew; a breakfast platter with eggs, hummus, and tabbouleh; and the eggs with grilled halloumi, all paired with house-made za'atar pita.

6. Casa Adela
66 Loisaida Avenue,
Alphabet City

The Puerto Rican Casa Adela has been an East Village mainstay since long before Alphabet City became a hot spot for trendy new restaurants and bars. The move here is the pernil—roast pork—or rotisserie chicken with a side of rice and beans and mofongo (mashed deep-fried green plantains). Note that it's cash only.

7. Cervo's
43 Canal Street,
Lower East Side

Cervo's takes the basic tenets of its older sibling, Bed-Stuy's Hart's (page 154)—briny flavors paired with an excellent natural wine and vermouth list—and gives it a Manhattan

35

stage at the heart of Dimes Square (page 78). It's hard to go wrong on this Spanish-Portuguese-inspired menu, but expect seafood like oysters, prawn heads, fried skate wings, and plenty of tinned fish.

8. Cocoron
16 Delancey Street, Lower East Side

Cocoron is one of the best places to get a bowl of soba noodles in Manhattan, an easy, casual dining option at the nexus of the Lower East Side and Nolita. No matter the season, there are dozens of variations of noodle options here, served chilled or in scalding hot soup. Likewise, this spot has something for every dietary restriction, with a comprehensive diagram that flags when dishes use ingredients like soy, sesame, tree nuts, meat, or more. Note that it's cash only, but there is an ATM inside.

9. Dhamaka
119 Delancey Street, Lower East Side

Located inside the Essex Market (page 43)—a market and food hall that relocated in recent years to new digs—Dhamaka is an Indian restaurant that has garnered serious fanfare for its daring menu, which includes items like goat kidney, lamb shank biryani, and whole rabbit. Despite the critical acclaim and higher price tag, it's a casual vibe. We recommend opting for the bar seating, which is easier to get as a walk-in.

10. El Castillo de Jagua
113 Rivington Street, Lower East Side

This Rivington Street Dominican diner (with a sibling on Grand Street) has remained a neighborhood lifeline since opening in 1968. The restaurant is known for its traditional dishes, like sancocho, a chicken soup with plantains and yucca, pork mofongo, rice and beans, and flan.

11. Estela
47 East Houston Street, Nolita

Estela, from star chef Ignacio Mattos (see also pages 12, 72, and 164), specializes in eclectic small plates that have become modern classics in their own right, including beef tartare with sunchokes, rich ricotta dumplings under a layer of razor-thin mushrooms, and fried black rice with squid.

12. Factory Tamal
34 Ludlow Street, Lower East Side

Fernando Lopez's take-out spot serves freshly made tamales out of locations on the Lower East Side and in the East Village. Flavors of the cornmeal-based treat steamed in corn husks range from a twenty-ingredient mole poblano to a salsa verde with chicken, bacon, and cheese, and a vegetarian portobello mushroom or zucchini version.

13. Golden Diner
123 Madison Street, Chinatown

Momofuku alum Sam Yoo runs this creative modern diner in the tiny area known as Two Bridges that's open morning through night. Its comfort food items tend to have a Pan-Asian spin: breakfast sandos served on scallion milk buns, a Thai-style cobb salad, and a chicken katsu club are just some of the offerings here.

14. Katz's Delicatessen
205 East Houston Street, Lower East Side

You likely know this pastrami palace from that "I'll have what she's having!" scene in *When Harry Met Sally*. Though overrun by tourists, it's still a neighborhood classic for its stacked sandwiches on rye, always with a pickle on the side. The neighborhood used to be known for its Jewish delicatessens, but these days Katz's is one of the last remaining. The lines here can be intimidating, but Katz's is open twenty-four hours on weekends, and it's much less busy late at night.

15. Kiki's

130 Division Street,
Lower East Side

Don't be confused by the Chinese characters out front: Kiki's serves Greek food. Its affordable food and wine carafes make it low-key one of the best restaurants in NYC. The move here is the chicken, which comes with soft potatoes in a creamy lemon sauce, gigante beans, fried zucchini chips, and one of the crunchiest Greek salads around. It's so popular that the team—which also owns the neighboring Forgtmenot—opened an identical restaurant across the street for spill-over seating.

16. Kopitiam

151 East Broadway,
Lower East Side

This order-at-the-counter Malaysian café is consistently on Eater best-of lists for its comforting all-day breakfast menu. The must-orders here are the kaya butter toast (kaya is a jam made with pandan and coconut) and the nasi lemak (a national dish of Malaysia, with crunchy fried anchovies, peanuts, and cool cucumbers over rice), as well as the spicy sesame noodles. Save room for sweets, like the kuih talam, layered with coconut milk and pandan cake.

17. Miss Lily's

109 Avenue A,
Alphabet City

A Caribbean restaurant where reggae and rum flow in equal measure, Miss Lily's on Avenue A is as vibrant as the packed streets of the East Village on a Friday night. As much as it can feel like a party restaurant, the food is great, too: jerk corn, codfish fritters, jerk salmon, and a Jamaican-style oxtail stew round out the menu.

18. Momofuku Noodle Bar

171 1st Avenue,
East Village

When David Chang opened this restaurant in 2004, it wasn't an immediate success. But soon enough, the restaurant—known for its big-swinging, playful takes on Asian food, in a restaurant blaring rock music—became a megahit. Now, Chang is a celebrity, known in equal measure for his food television appearances as for his cooking. Chang has so many restaurants, with varying perspectives, that it'd be hard to check them all off in one visit. For a taste of where it all started, check out the original noodle shop.

19. Nom Wah Tea Parlor

13 Doyers Street,
Chinatown

Considered to be the first dim sum parlor in Chinatown, Nom Wah Tea Parlor has been up and running since 1920. Its signature yellow-and-red exterior beckons in thousands of tourists each year for staples like shrimp shumai, roast pork buns, and pan-fried pork dumplings (shown below). Lines run long, but luckily there is a Nolita location if you can't get in here.

20. Punjabi Deli

114 East 1st Street,
East Village

A known favorite stop among yellow taxi drivers in the city for thirty years, Punjabi Deli is essentially a bodega with a hot bar. Ten dollars in cash is plenty of money to get a plate of rice with veggie sides like chana masala (spiced chickpeas) or samosas. Post up on a

bench outside with a paper plate and watch the customers line up across the street at Katz's (page 36).

21. Scarr's Pizza
35 Orchard Street,
Lower East Side
Located on a section of Orchard Street filled with fun shops and bars, Scarr Pimentel's shop really sets itself apart from other new-fangled slice shops for milling its own grains, something nearly unheard-of in the city. His slices are routinely described as some of the best you can get anywhere, and accordingly attract long lines. Luckily, you can now make a reservation to avoid the wait.

22. Shu Jiao Fu Zhou
295 Grand Street,
Chinatown
One of the best meals in Manhattan for the budget-strapped is pan-fried or steamed pork dumplings at Shu Jiao Fu Zhou, where a large-sized dumpling order costs less than $5. But fans also know to order the peanut butter noodles, filling for under $3.

23. Spicy Village
68 Forsyth Street,
Chinatown
Spicy Village is a BYOB Chinese restaurant known for its spicy big-tray chicken and hand-pulled noodles. It's casual—lines run deep, but service moves quickly, and smaller parties sit at communal tables.

24. Superiority Burger
119 Avenue A,
Alphabet City
Formerly a tiny take-out spot on East Ninth Street, in 2023 Superiority Burger relocated to a full-service restaurant, in the former locaton of OG East Village diner Odessa. In its new digs, Superiority Burger keeps the spirit of the New York classic with comfort food staples that are all vegetarian and sometimes accidentally vegan, too. Fans are rabid here, so expect wait times.

25. Taiwan Pork Chop House
3 Doyers Street,
Chinatown
Yes, there's a lengthy menu running to typical Cantonese, a few Sichuan, and bedrock Taiwanese fare, but most diners sit down to one of the two specialties of the house, offered with abundant quantities of rice and pickled mustard greens. It can be a difficult decision: the legendary thin-cut pork chops with a sweet glaze, or the bulbous chicken leg, briny and delicious. Both are equally good.

26. Thai Diner
186 Mott Street,
Nolita
No matter the time of day, Thai Diner serves up comforting plates of Thai food with diner-y twists: cabbage rolls, creamy coconut curry khao soi, and breakfast wraps served on roti are crowd favorites. Don't miss the kid-friendly coconut-cloaked ice cream sundae or the coffee cake made to look like a little monster.

27. The Tin Building
96 South Street,
Financial District

In a project nearly a decade in the making, celebrity chef Jean-Georges Vongerichten has restored this historic South Street Seaport building (shown above) and turned it into a high-end food court—though calling it such doesn't quite do it justice. Inside the fifty-three-thousand-square-foot marketplace there are six full-service restaurants, four bars, six counters, retail, and private dining, with food options that run the gamut from egg sandwiches to Chinese food, dosas, vegetarian fare, and a bakery; all use the same top-tier sourcing employed in Vongerichten's other restaurants.

28. Uncle Lou
73 Mulberry Street,
Chinatown

Uncle Lou is one of several restaurants remaking Cantonese food in Chinatown, taking traditional recipes, kicking them up a notch with better ingredients, and serving them ceremoniously on big round tables with turntables in the middle for easy sharing. Chef's specials are called lo wah kiu ("the old timers") and include steak cooked with chives, vegetarian tofu-skin wraps, and homestyle chenpi duck with mandarin-orange-peel sauce.

29. Veselka
144 2nd Avenue,
East Village

While Veselka is no longer the twenty-four-hour establishment it once was, morning, noon, or night it stays packed. The Ukrainian diner has been a backdrop to countless movies and television shows, known for serving up pierogi, borscht, and chicken schnitzel in a dining room that has served people from all walks of life since 1954.

30. Wildair
142 Orchard Street,
Lower East Side

Wildair, a natural wine bar with an equally compelling savory menu, is known for its tight list of small plates and dessert menu, as well as its sceney downtown feel. The team also consistently hosts donut pop-ups, so follow the restaurant on Instagram to stay up-to-date with events.

31. Wu's Wonton King
165 East Broadway,
Lower East Side

Located where Chinatown meets the Lower East Side, Wu's Wonton King is a Cantonese favorite, at once casual and celebratory, with a generous BYOB policy, a favorite among food-industry folks who like to flex by bringing natural wine bottles to share. Neighbors new and old flock here to eat Beijing duck on large round tables shrouded in white tablecloths. It's best for groups. Call via phone to make a reservation, or to preorder a suckling whole pig, but usually there's no trouble getting a table here.

39

32. Yellow Rose

102 3rd Avenue,
East Village

Over the past couple of years New York has undergone a flour tortilla renaissance, with Tex-Mex Yellow Rose at the forefront. Try their bean and cheese taco, migas breakfast taco, or carne guisada (stewed beef with a dried chile sauce). Yellow Rose also offers plenty of daily-changing specials, including salads with a tomatillo dressing, queso fundido, Frito pie, and one of the best sheet cakes this city has to offer. Be sure to try the margarita, especially good here, but also drinks like the Cherry Coke cocktail.

33. Yi Ji Shi Mo

88 Elizabeth Street,
Chinatown

Since 2019, Manhattan's Chinatown has been experiencing a rice roll boom on its streets, a dish long seen at dim sum parlors. One of our favorites is Yi Ji Shi Mo, a perfect place to get a hearty meal for less than $10. In truth, though, nearly everywhere in Chinatown you turn there are great rice rolls to be found, such as at Tonii's, Joe's Steam Rice Roll, and so many others.

QR CODES for our online guides to **DOWNTOWN EAST** neighborhoods:

CHINATOWN

EAST VILLAGE

LITTLE ITALY

LOWER EAST SIDE

NOLITA

DOWNTOWN EAST
SHOPPING

The blend of old and new that defines so much of New York is starkly apparent in this area. In the East Village, a revolving door of businesses caters to each new generation of college students. Yet the grit that made it a hub for artists and musicians decades ago remains, along with lingering reminders that a part of the neighborhood was once known as Little Ukraine and another part is considered Little Tokyo. Farther south, shops that served twentieth-century Jewish immigrants now draw tourists, while modern boutiques attract the city's most stylish. And just to the west, Chinatown's restaurants and shops endure, as they have for more than a century.

1. Bonnie Slotnick Cookbooks

28 East 2nd Street,
East Village

Bonnie Slotnick has been selling cookbooks for more than twenty-five years, although not from this exact location. The shop was so beloved by its community that when Slotnick lost her Greenwich Village lease in 2014, the set of siblings who own this building offered her the opportunity to move east. Today, cookbook collectors can shop for rare and antiquarian cookbooks—from vintage baking pamphlets to historic cloth-bound tomes—down the steps of a nineteenth-century building on an East Village side street.

2. Coming Soon

53 Canal Street,
Lower East Side

Design fans should make their way to the corner of Canal and Orchard Streets, an area known slangily as Dimes Square (so named for a nearby restaurant and the hip clientele who flock to it and the surrounding businesses). Coming Soon fits right in with its of-the-moment furniture and home café. The kitchenware in particular consistently delights with a selection of colorful drinkware, irreverent place mats, and even designy kitchen sponges that are more fun than a sponge has any right to be.

3. Despaña

408 Broome Street,
Nolita

At Despaña, tinned fish has always been en vogue. Beginning its life as a chorizo factory in Jackson Heights, Queens, in 1971, the brand has since grown to include this Soho café and grocery store stocked full of Spanish imports, including cheeses, olives, cured meats, and the aforementioned tins upon tins of conservas. Despaña Vinos y Más right next door sells wines, sherries, and, as it says in the name, more in the realm of Spanish drinks, with a focus on both traditional winemaking and the next generation of must-know Spanish vintners.

4. Di Palo's Fine Foods

200 Grand Street,
Little Italy

Di Palo's Fine Foods is perhaps the most recognizable of the specialty shops in Manhattan's Little Italy. Behind the marble counter, now run by the fifth generation, cases hold Italian cheeses (the fresh mozzarella is the cheese that started it all) and cured meats, while shelves around the edge of the shop display dried pastas and canned tomatoes. Down the center there's room for a line to form, a not-unusual occurrence, so for leisurely sampling before you buy, it's best to visit at an off hour.

5. Economy Candy
108 Rivington Street,
Lower East Side

Economy Candy has been supplying the Lower East Side with sugary treats since 1937, and when you step into the packed-to-the-gills store, the history is clear. On near-overflowing shelves, you'll find the most popular candy from every decade of Economy's tenure, from candy cigarettes to Fun Dip, alongside international offerings like Turkish delight and Chupa Chups. But Economy isn't just for the kids at heart looking for a sweet nostalgia trip; it's also sure to have whatever candy the actual kids are raving about, whether it's gummy sushi or the newest Kit-Kat flavor. They also now have a second location in Chelsea Market (page 18).

6. Essex Market and the Market Line
88 Essex Street,
Lower East Side

Essex Market has been serving the Lower East Side community from the corner of Essex and Delancey Streets since the nineteenth century. But in 2019, it moved across the intersection to the Essex Crossing development, where it shares space with the new Market Line and food hall. Upstairs, shop for groceries and specialty foods from longtime Essex Market vendors, and then head downstairs to visit some more recent neighborhood institutions, like Peoples Wine, the wine shop and bar from Wildair (page 39) chefs Jeremiah Stone and Fabián von Hauske-Valtierra along with Daryl Nuhn.

7. John Derian Company Inc.
6 East 2nd Street,
East Village

Designer John Derian now has five shops in New York and New England, but this is the original, opened in 1995 to sell the decoupaged tabletop accessories that've become his signature. Alongside plates and paperweights adorned with butterflies, flowers, and other images seemingly straight from a naturalist guidebook, find vintage and antique tableware as well as collections from contemporary designers that fit right in with Derian's brand of modern opulence.

8. The Meadow
240 Mulberry Street,
Nolita

Originally from Portland, Oregon, the Meadow is a specialty food shop with three distinct focuses: salt, chocolate, and bitters. Chocolate—350 bars of it from at least 75 purveyors—lines floor-to-ceiling shelves along one wall, while bitters and salt dominate the other half of the narrow space. Meadow owner Mark Bitterman keeps his own line of salt in stock alongside big Himalayan blocks and copies of *Salted*, the James Beard Award–winning book that solidified his expertise on the matter.

9. Nalata Nalata
2 Extra Place,
East Village

In a serene space on Extra Place, the couple behind Nalata Nalata present a tight collection of home goods, with a focus on highlighting Japanese design. Befitting the gallery-like room, every object is display-worthy, from smaller items like patterned tenugui cloths and architectural bamboo spatulas (both perfect for packing in a suitcase) to the heftier ceramic donabes and iron pans.

10. The Pickle Guys
357 Grand Street,
Lower East Side

There was a time when Lower East Side pickle vendors were a dime a dozen. Now, only the Pickle Guys carries on the tradition with a store devoted to barrel-cured pickles. There's a variety of pickled cucumbers, naturally, but these guys are also pickling tomatoes, peppers, turnips, watermelon, pineapple, and more. If you'd like to try before you buy, Diller,

the Pickle Guys' snack bar next door, serves the shop's bread-and-butter pickles fried in portable cardboard cones.

11. Russ & Daughters
179 East Houston Street,
Lower East Side

After braving the crowds waiting for bagels, you can shop the Jewish foods that have made this appetizing store such an enduring piece of Lower East Side history. Smoked fish may not be the most portable of souvenirs, but you can still take home some dried fruit, sweets (think jelly rings, halva, rugelach, and the like), and tins of caviar, or a selection of Russ & Daughters merch. For a

sit-down brunch, visit Russ & Daughters Cafe down the street.

12. SOS Chefs
104 Avenue B,
Alphabet City

The final "S" in SOS Chefs stands for "Spices," not "Souls," and that should tell you everything you need to know about how owner Atef Boulaabi thinks about her stock. SOS Chefs is a specialty shop for obscure ingredients—spices, yes, but also truffles, honey, freeze-dried powders, vinegars, and much, much more. On the website, Boulaabi explains that the product list grew through answering years of chef requests, and while it remains a go-to for

the professionals, the passionate home cook is just as welcome in the cozy East Village storefront.

13. Stick With Me Sweets
202A Mott Street,
Nolita

On a Nolita corner, Stick With Me Sweets doles out the prettiest bonbons in the city, but Susanna Yoon's creations offer much more than good looks. Each chocolate contains expertly layered flavors, often inspired by much larger desserts, like the calamansi meringue pie or black-and-white cookie bonbons. Others take broader inspiration, such as the classic "New York, New York," filled with candied pecans, pretzels, and caramel. They're an ideal gift, packaged in a storybook-themed box with a booklet to identify each flavor, but don't leave without buying a bonbon—or several—for yourself.

14. Union Square Greenmarket
Union Square Park

Manhattan's premier farmers' market stretches from the southwest to northeast corners of Union Square Park every Monday, Wednesday, Friday, and Saturday, year-round. Among the stalls of farm-fresh fruits, vegetables, and flowers, you'll find cheese and dairy products, baked goods, jams, syrups, whiskey, and any number of other potential gifts or snacks for the plane ride home. Go before nine A.M. for shorter lines and to see local chefs pick up the farm half of their farm-to-table preparations.

15. Wing On Wo & Co.
26 Mott Street,
Chinatown

Wing On Wo & Co. holds the distinction of being the oldest store in Manhattan's Chinatown. First opened in the 1890s to sell Chinese pantry goods, five generations later, the focus has shifted to ceramics, from chopstick rests and tea sets to hand-painted decorative plates. And the shop's most recent owner, Mei Lum, sees its purpose as extending beyond selling housewares, starting the W.O.W. Project,

a community initiative dedicated to preserving Chinatown's creative culture, in part by inviting artists to design the Wing On Wo & Co. window.

16. Yunhong Chopsticks
50 Mott Street,
Chinatown

Chopsticks are perhaps the easiest gift to bring back from Manhattan's Chinatown—they'll fit right into a bag without risk of incurring damage—and there's no better place to shop for them than Yunhong. In fact, there's little else in the tiny shop. But this doesn't mean there isn't plenty to browse, with hundreds of varieties of the essential utensil at any price point or design you desire, including a particularly adorable selection of training chopsticks.

BEYOND RESTAURANTS

Coffee Shops
Abraço
Black Fox Coffee Co.
La Cabra
Suited

Bars
Amor Y Amargo
Attaboy
Bar Goto
The Dead Rabbit
Death & Co
Double Chicken Please
Holiday Cocktail
    Lounge
Lucy's
McSorley's Old Ale
    House

Bakeries
Café d'Avignon
From Lucie
Harper's Bread House
Lady Wong
Librae Bakery
Raf's
Smor Bakery
Tai Pan Bakery

Ice Cream/Sweets
Caleta
Il Laboratorio del
    Gelato
Meet Fresh
The Original Chinatown
    Ice Cream Factory
Sundaes and Cones

NYC ESSENTIALS

By Ryan Sutton

PIZZA

Christopher Moltisanti on *The Sopranos*, played with hammy gusto by Michael Imperioli, was a philanderer, hypocrite, mob captain, failed thespian, drug dealer, dog killer, waiter killer, and really big Lindsay Lohan fan. And yet he famously uttered the following wisdom: "Don't disrespect the pizza parlor." Amen. Even in a fictional fantasy world where murder is a way of life, the pizzeria—first brought to us by Italian immigrants in the early twentieth century—is holy, a secular church of sorts.

Nowhere in New York City, New Jersey, or Long Island is there a culinary establishment more ubiquitous or affordable to all, and nowhere else in the country is there such a wide swath of pizza options. With relative ease you can find classic slices, 'roni cup squares, Roman squares, Sicilian squares, al taglio style, Staten Island pies with crusts thinner than most microprocessors, fancy Neapolitan pies, new-school bakery-style slices, and Caribbean slices laden with so much curried oxtail the pizza appears to be wearing army camouflage.

When exploring the city's best pizzas, keep the following three rules in mind. First, you can spend a lot of money on truffled pies at chic restaurants, but pizza doesn't have to be expensive. Unlike steak or caviar, the cost is not necessarily a reflection of the quality. Second, pie-only spots, while great, aren't necessarily better than slice spots, which are undergoing a serious revolution in quality. Third, be purposeful in your pizza search. While you can encounter decent-enough pizza by walking into a random slice spot, a lot of folks are doing some cool and ambitious stuff. This guide will help your search in that regard.

Old-school slice shop

Sam Raimi gave Peter Parker a job at **Joe's Pizza** on Carmine Street in *Spider-Man 2*, because Joe's, opened by Pino "Joe" Pozzuoli, in 1975, serves an excellent example of the quintessentially foldable New York slice. Cooks stretch and toss the dough before coating it with a lightly spiced tomato sauce and a low-moisture mozzarella, which holds up better to the long gas oven cooking times than fresh mozz. The result is a style of slice that epitomizes, to many, the tri-state pizza-eating experience. The bread is sturdy, filling, and faintly crisp; the tomato sauce is more sweet than tangy; and the cheese is salty and stretchy, allowing for long, satisfying, mouth-burning pulls. And of course, it radiates that handsome orange hue. Joe's might be one of the best, but you can find versions of this style at scores of pizzerias in and around New York City.

Joe's Pizza
7 Carmine Street, West Village, Manhattan

New-school slices

A newer crop of bakers are tinkering with classic recipes to push pizza into the future, often using high hydration ratios, natural leavening, and long fermentations to create lighter, more distinctly flavored and bubblier crusts. While pizzas at older spots can sometimes feel a touch leaden during digestion, the naturally low gluten levels at these venues often means you can eat two or three slices without feeling too many ill effects. High-quality ingredients also allow for creations that aren't so much generically cheesy, salty, and stretchy as they are lucid

expressions of milky mozzarella, bright tomatoes, and pristine toppings. This is pizza as a platform, a bully pulpit for larger ideas.

L'Industrie's burrata slice is a prime example of this style. Chef Massimo Laveglia lets cool, creamy curds mingle with warm tomato sauce on a slice so feathery it would surely blow away if a neighborhood cat sneezed nearby. Just as nimble is the vegan tomato slice at **F&F**, sporting a layer of fruit so lean it seems to be spray-painted on the crust. Find a more nostalgic approach to new-school pizza at **Scarr's** on the Lower East Side (for an airy, chewy crust paired with natural wines, page 38), **Paulie Gee's Slice Shop** in Greenpoint (for a mysterious smokiness), or **Fini** in Williamsburg (for a white slice slathered in a nacho cheese–like mixture of fontina and Parmesan—and a scattering of lemon zest).

L'Industrie Pizzeria
254 South 2nd Street, Williamsburg, Brooklyn

F&F Pizzeria
459 Court Street, Carroll Gardens, Brooklyn

Paulie Gee's Slice Shop
110 Franklin Street, Greenpoint, Brooklyn

Fini Pizza
305 Bedford Avenue, Williamsburg, Brooklyn

Classic Neapolitan pies

A classic Neapolitan pizza is typically just a few bare-bones ingredients garnishing a puffy disc of dough, all cooked for no more than ninety seconds in a wood-fired oven. Expect a slightly soupy center at times, and a mildly floppy interior crust—this is the only time you can eat pizza with cutlery in New York.

Anthony Mangieri, the fastidious pizzaiolo of **Una Pizza Napoletana**, makes one of the city's most heralded versions, shaping his naturally leavened dough like the wheel on a 1957 Chevy: puffy and fat at the rim and thinner in the middle. A marinara pie is nothing more than fresh milled tomatoes—umami-rich and tart—made extra savory thanks to the heat of the oven and the herbal punch of good oregano. The margherita, of course, includes little dots of ultra-creamy mozzarella, softening the blow of the piquant fruit. Also consider the estimable versions at **Ops** (also see Leo,

page 131), which offers a pulpier marinara and a slightly less pillowy crust than Una.

For a more modern take on Neapolitan pies—without the soupy center—**Roberta's** (page 132) ranks among the top choices, especially thanks to its wide array of toppings. Try the Axl Rosenberg, a mix of mushrooms, soppressata, jalapeños, and garlic, or the Beastmaster, a funky blend of mozzarella, pork sausage, and gorgonzola.

Una Pizza Napoletana
175 Orchard Street, Lower East Side, Manhattan

Ops
346 Himrod Street, Bushwick, Brooklyn

Roman squares

Sullivan Street Bakery (page 15) is where you go when you're in the mood for pizza as a light breakfast or midday snack with a cup of coffee. Acclaimed baker Jim Lahey serves his pristine squares, the kind one might find in Rome, starting at twelve P.M., using a no-knead overnight bianca dough made from winter wheat harvested in the Dakotas. He garnishes the slices—no thicker than a few sheets of paper— with milled

tomatoes, 75 percent domestic and 25 percent from San Marzano. You eat the squares at room temperature, letting the chewy bread and its hint of sweetness act as a foil for the bright, vegetal fruit; call it a year-round ode to summer. Also try the more filling slices, with cauliflower and anchovy or mandoline-sliced potatoes and rosemary.

The Jersey powerhouses

The Garden State has long been a US pizza capital, but two new-school spots in Jersey City are rightly drawing a new set of pilgrims from New York and beyond to experience some of the country's best pies. At the **Bread and Salt** Italian bakery, Rick Easton crafts Roman-style pizzas—imagine the shape of a paddle—so expertly that the slices sometimes seem to flake and pull apart like a stretchy pain au chocolat. His high-hydration, long-fermentation process results in what might be the city's airiest slices. Easton has since trimmed a multitude of toppings to a minimalist menu of rossa (no cheese) or a sublime margherita with tart, umami-rich Gustarosso tomatoes, a backdrop for a milky Lancaster mozzarella.

For a more full-service experience, consider **Razza**. Here, Dan Richer serves wood-fired pies that blend the wispy thinness of round

Roman pies, a cracker-like rim crunch, and a more forgiving chew. Those lucky enough to visit in the warmer months might encounter a pie with fresh Jersey corn and spicy fermented chile paste, or the seasonal summer margherita, a blend of creamy Sussex County mozz and fresh crushed tomatoes—versus the excellent and more tart canned ones Richer uses the rest of the year.

Bread and Salt
435 Palisade Avenue, Jersey City

Razza
275/277 Grove Street, Jersey City

Surprising slices

David Poran and Michael Bergemann's **Corner Slice** bakery, located within sight of the *Intrepid* aircraft carrier on the far West Side, has reliably sold some of the city's best grandma-esque square slices since it opened in 2017. What's more surprising, however, is witnessing the duo's high-wire breadmaking—long fermentation applied to freshly milled spelt and durum—used on that beloved New York trash slice: the buffalo chicken pie. Orange cubes of tangy, chile-drenched meat sit atop a milky layer of mozz and creamy ranch. It looks as heavy as a casserole, yet the bread underneath is filled with bubbly air pockets; this loaded Buffalo slice is, against all odds, strikingly light. Also be sure to try the clam slice, an occasional special that blends butter, brine, and chiles to a masterful effect.

Randy Mclaren's **Cuts & Slices** is such a refreshing counterpoint to the city's largely Italian and American pizza scene. This Caribbean-style slice spot offers jerk shrimp slices and curiously light oxtail slices, slicked with rich brown sauce, sweet chile sauce, or a forest-green curry sauce. The curried slice is particularly majestic, bursting with heady notes of garlic and onion, while the beef flaunts its ample and sticky gelatins.

Corner Slice
600 11th Avenue, Hell's Kitchen, Manhattan

Cuts & Slices
93 Howard Avenue, Bed-Stuy, Brooklyn

Staten Island–style vodka pies

Joe & Pat's has been serving round, thin-crust pies in Staten Island since the 1960s and in the East Village since 2018. How thin are they? You don't so much eat these pies as you inhale them; the cracker-like crusts recall matzoh. The signature offering is the vodka pie, with gobs of creamy mozzarella intermingling with sweet, tomato-laced sauce. Most diners could wolf down the ten-inch version in just a few minutes. For something more substantial, sexy, and hip—call

it Staten Island pizza for millennials—swing by **Rubirosa** in Nolita, founded by a member of the larger Joe & Pat's family. That venue's pies are larger, with a touch more chew, while the vodka sauce flaunts a bit more tomato-based fruitiness.

Joe & Pat's
1758 Victory Boulevard, Staten Island

Rubirosa
235 Mulberry Street, Nolita, Manhattan

Sicilian squares

New Yorkers can find puffy, deep-dish, Sicilian-style squares at most neighborhood pizzerias, but one in particular rises above the crowd. In Brooklyn, **L&B Spumoni Gardens** (page 154) famously applies its sweet tomato sauce over the cheese, letting the topping act as a slightly soupy and pulpy counterpoint to the crisp crust, which often sports a dusting of Pecorino Romano baked in.

Coal-fired pies

Gennaro Lombardi, an immigrant from Naples, reportedly applied for and received the city's first pizza license in 1905, giving **Lombardi's** claim to the title of the first pizzeria in the United States. And while pizza authorities suggest the true history is a bit more complicated, the coal oven pies of Lombardi's—there were no gas ovens back then—still draw throngs of tourists to this day. What's more, the founders of other historic New York coal-oven pizzerias, including **Totonno's** of Coney Island, **John's of Bleecker Street** (page 14), and **Patsy's** of East Harlem, all reportedly trained at Lombardi's (while the founder of the coal-fired Grimaldi's worked at Patsy's). Some might argue coal-fired pies are little different from wood-fired pies—and that some of these venues are past their prime—but it's indisputable that these institutions remain a vital part of the city's pizza culture.

Lombardi's
32 Spring Street, Nolita, Manhattan

Totonno's
1524 Neptune Avenue, Coney Island, Brooklyn

Patsy's
2287 1st Avenue, East Harlem, Manhattan

Chicago-style tavern pies

Many folks associate Chicago-style pizza with the soupy, gooey, deep-dish-style casserole pies, but Windy City residents are more likely to enjoy tavern pizza on a regular basis. Anyone who's ever had Domino's thin crust pizza essentially knows this fine pizza format, which is quite rare in New York. Accordingly, those craving tavern pies should swing by **Emmett's on Grove** in the West Village, where cooks run dough through a sheeter, bake it in an electric oven, and cut it into cute little squares. The Hot Papi, layered with tons of jalapeño peppers, red onions, paprika ranch dressing, and pepperoni, is loaded so heavily, it's akin to a giant plate of loaded nachos.

Emmett's on Grove
39 Grove Street, West Village, Manhattan

Crispy, crunchy, filling Detroit pies

For folks craving the rich, filling bliss of Detroit-style rectangular pizza, Matt Hyland's growing chain of **Emmy Squared** pizzerias are usually the right call. The resident chefs bake a thick layer of dough in an oil-filled pan, letting the bottom take on a golden-brown hue, while a layer of mozz around the edges fries up, taking on the texture of a Parmesan crisp. This isn't a snack pizza, but rather a hefty meal with complex textures ranging from soft and bready to wonderfully crunchy. Try the pie with spicy banana peppers and ranch for a puckery, cooling sensation.

Emmy Squared
Multiple locations

Fancy pizza

New York's best pizzerias are largely affordable take-out affairs, but for those who prefer a more luxe sit-down experience, we have that, too. Jean-Georges Vongerichten has long hawked a spendy black truffle pizza, letting the complex earthiness of the fungi mingle with the pronounced sweetness of his whole-wheat dough; he sells this at a number of venues, perhaps the best of which is **ABC Kitchen**. Dan Kluger, a Vongerichten acolyte, also sells a masterpiece of a whole-wheat Sicilian-style pizza at **Loring Place**; the crust is so feathery yet crisp it seems to defy most laws of physics.

ABC Kitchen
35 East 18th Street, Union Square, Manhattan

Loring Place
21 West 8th Street, Greenwich Village, Manhattan

MODERN KOREAN

If you splurge on a single fancy meal in New York, make it modern Korean. One can of course splurge extraordinarily well on other cuisines (see page 62 for more ideas); New York boasts well-known fancy French spots, dizzyingly expensive sushi counters, new Nordic temples, exorbitant pasta dens on Billionaires' Row, Mexican hot spots hawking ethereal moles, and Chinese seafood halls where a group can easily drop $700 or more on king crab. Thing is, it's not hard to find similar venues across the United States. But outside of the East Asian peninsula, no other city flaunts a more robust collection of upscale modern Korean spots than New York.

The scene offers cutting-edge, contemporary, and high-end fare. Tabletop grill spots mix Korean beef barbecue with the indulgences of a classic old-school steak house; omakase hand roll venues tip their hats as much to Japanese temaki as

Korean kimbap; and Korean tasting-menu venues top their charcoal-grilled skewers with bubbly French foams.

The debut of **Jungsik** in Tribeca in 2011, a few years after a Seoul flagship of the same name opened, helped launch the posh side of the modern Korean movement in New York, giving expats a fancy taste of home while introducing certain New York gourmands to a style of chic Asian dining they might not have been previously familiar with.

Fast-forward to today, and modern Korean restaurants aren't just modern Manhattan or Brooklyn restaurants; they are what fancy French restaurants used to be. They are, along with New York's burgeoning sushi scene, the single most salient feature of the city's fine-dining community. And they occupy the creative vanguard of New York gastronomy—a reality that comes at a time when South Korea's status as a global exporter of all forms of groundbreaking movies, music, TV shows, luxury cars, and other cultural totems is stronger than ever. In fact, those who mourn the loss of New York's modernist spots of the aughts—Tailor, WD-50, and Varietal—should swing by a place like **Joomak Banjum**, which serves dishes like duck legs with donuts and funky raclette ice cream.

Or they can drop by **Atoboy** for dishes like injeolmi rice cakes that have been transformed into mousse.

Caviar, wagyu, and truffles, those increasingly universal (if tired) signifiers of opulence, often make their way onto these menus, but modern Korean spots also tend to show off a more open-minded approach to luxury. Part of the equation is that these restaurants are willing to push the culinary envelope a bit further than their European American and Japanese counterparts, but sometimes the chefs simply want to riff on the traditional foodways of South Korea in their own fancy way.

At **Atomix** (page 69), the kitchen serves ingredients rarely seen in New York fine-dining palaces, like sea cucumbers, jiggly jellyfish, and salted belt fish innards. At **Cote** (page 69), a Korean American steak house in Flatiron, chef David Shim offers an omakase that intersperses common cuts of meat with decidedly uncommon ones, like the obscenely marbled beef in between a cow's ribs, and chuck flap. And while one will find predictably tasty wagyu galbi at **Oiji Mi**, chef Brian Kim's chic restaurant in Flatiron, the kitchen has featured jook, or porridge, studded with abalone and pickled ramps on its tasting menu.

Banchan, small communal side dishes like kimchi and dried

anchovy, frequently make a welcome appearance at upscale modern Korean spots. At **Mari**, a hand roll omakase restaurant in Hell's Kitchen, those side dishes remain quite lean and classic, like a few slices of vinegar-pickled cauliflower or soy-pickled jicama. But at **Jua**, a wood-fired tasting menu joint in Flatiron, the chef prepares his banchan with such lean precision it's as if he's re-creating a modernist sundial from ancient Babylonia.

These tastings generally fall anywhere from low- to mid-three figures, with Atomix and Jungsik at the higher end. At the latter, some of the best dishes can also be found on the (expensive) à la carte bar menu.

Here's a hint: Drop by Jungsik for dessert, particularly for the "carrot." The ultra-creative item is presented, Cédric Grolet–style, as an actual carrot you pull from the dirt. As it turns out, the trompe l'oeil confection is actually a clever blend of carrot cake and black tea ice cream. For a slightly more low-key approach to modernist Korean sweets, pre-order to avoid the hourlong wait at **Lysée** in Flatiron, a self-proclaimed "gallery of confections." Eunji Lee, formerly the executive pastry chef at, you guessed it, Jungsik, lists her daily bill of fare on the "our collections" section of the Lysée website and charges what you'd expect for a boutique that would make an Apple store look shabby by comparison. If it's not sold out, order the corn cake, which doesn't so much look like an actual corn husk as an exaggerated video game version of one, with giant yellow kernels and edible leaves made from grilled corn cream and corn mousse.

Jungsik
2 Harrison Street, Tribeca, Manhattan

Joomak Banjum
312 5th Avenue, Koreatown, Manhattan

Atoboy
43 East 28th Street, Nomad, Manhattan

Oiji Mi
17 West 19th Street, Flatiron, Manhattan

Mari
679 9th Avenue, Hell's Kitchen, Manhattan

Jua
36 East 22nd Street, Flatiron, Manhattan

Lysée
44 East 21st Street, Flatiron, Manhattan

CENTRAL ASIAN CUISINE

Folks who aren't from the former Soviet Union might not associate Central Asian fare with the New York experience as much as they think of pizza or pastrami. Yet make no mistake: Eating a pumpkin-stuffed pastry samsa on the Coney Island boardwalk, or riding the Q train with a floppy, buttery fatir, a Persian sweet bread, is as New York as eating a hot dog and fried clams at nearby **Nathan's** (page 155).

The Big Apple is the de facto home of Central Asian cuisine in the United States. That's all the more true for the diverse foodways of Uzbekistan; at least 100,000 New York residents have direct or ancestral ties to the region. Most are Bukharans, a historic Jewish population who fled persecution as the Soviet Union collapsed; they largely settled in Rego Park and Forest Hills. Walk up and down Sixty-Third Street in Queens and you'll encounter fine kosher restaurants and bakeries. Expect to hear Russian, English, Uzbek, Tajik, and Bukharan in any single room. Or swing by Manhattan's Diamond District for **Taam Tov**, a gem of a Midtown lunch spot known for its fine shurpa (beef soup) and bakhsh, a verdant rice pilaf with chicken and parsley.

Uzbekistan's Muslims, in turn, have predominantly taken up residence in Sheepshead Bay, Ditmas Park, Kensington, and elsewhere in South Brooklyn, thousands of them having availed themselves of a special visa program to flee economic hardship at home. Many of these venues are halal.

The oft-packed **Nargis Cafe** in Sheepshead Bay merits a special trip alone. But those who stroll farther north will encounter scores more Uzbek restaurants, such as **Arzu Palace** and **Sherdor**. And if folks walk farther south to Brighton Beach, a historic stronghold for Russian speakers, they'll pass by **Brighton Tandir**, one of the city's best Uzbek bakeries, as well as **Tashkent Supermarket**, where the two-hundred-tray hot buffet can feel like the F train during rush hour. There patrons scoop up braided Kazakh meat pies, pumpkin-stuffed samsa, and piles of airy Kyrgyz norin noodles that disappear so fast they almost seem to melt like ice cream scoops on a sweltering summer's day.

No country's cuisine is a monolith, but Uzbekistan benefits from a particularly diverse gastronomic heritage. Some of the oldest traditions are Turkic and Persian. One thinks of tandoor-cooked naan—pressed into the shape of old-timey pneumatic wheels—or plov, rice pilafs that are simmered here (instead of steamed), with the grains soaking up the flavor of raisins, sweet yellow carrots, and garlicky lamb broth. Korean food also plays a notable role in the country—Stalin deported nearly 175,000 Koreans from Russia's Far East to Central Asia in 1937—which explains the ubiquity of morkovcha, a quick, spicy kimchi of carrots with garlic, cilantro, and chile.

Beef and poultry are widely available in modern Uzbekistan, but mutton is the country's historic meat of choice, a product of the old nomadic traditions of the Central Asian steppe. Fatty lamb ribs, heady with cumin and meaty funk, are a particular specialty at most local spots, but those who appreciate Uzbekistan's nose-to-tail ethos should swing by **Cheburechnaya** for lamb heart, lamb testicles, and, most important, kurdyuk—pure tail fat that's been grilled to a sweet crisp.

Scores of local Central Asian restaurants serve Uyghur fare— usually lagman noodles, a staple dish in Uzbekistan— but New York has its own supply of stand-alone Uyghur spots.

Temur Yazova helps run one of the city's oldest and best Uyghur spots, **Kashkar Cafe** (page 154) in Brighton Beach, a halal restaurant that serves plates of pan-fried noodles, chuchvara, and yutaza say, pools of lamb and sauce meant to be mopped up with steamed dumplings. **Nurlan** in Queens, by contrast, devotes more care to lagman. Unlike the soupier Uzbek version, Nurlan prepares its lagman as a plate of firm, long, hand-stretched noodles, with a generous ladle of lamb stew on top.

Taam Tov
41 West 47th Street,
Midtown West, Manhattan

Nargis Cafe
1655 Sheepshead Bay Road,
Sheepshead Bay, Brooklyn

Arzu Palace
2390 Coney Island Avenue,
Sheepshead Bay, Brooklyn

Sherdor
1917 Avenue U, Sheepshead Bay, Brooklyn

Brighton Tandir
504 Bridge Beach Avenue,
Brighton Beach, Brooklyn

Tashkent Supermarket
713 Brighton Beach Avenue,
Brighton Beach, Brooklyn

Cheburechnaya
9209 63rd Drive, Rego Park, Queens

Nurlan
43-39 Main Street, Flushing, Queens

STEAK AND OTHER MEATS

Steak houses and chophouses are among New York's oldest, most recognizable, and most popular restaurants. **Gallaghers** (page 70) is practically a youngster, having opened nearly a century ago in 1927. **Keens** (page 71), famous for its pipe collection, scotches, and mutton, debuted in 1885. **Old Homestead** has been around since the 1860s. And **Peter Luger** (page 132) which opened in Brooklyn in 1887, still draws never-ending crowds, despite being battered by negative reviews from food critics in recent years.

Indeed, New York remains one of the best places in the country to eat red meat, be it dry-aged strips the size of small dogs or hunks of lamb as weighty as kettlebells. But here's the thing: You're not *always* best off eating steak at steak houses. Sometimes they offer fantastic pleasures of yesteryear, but sometimes they serve as bastions of underseasoned, overpriced, poorly cooked meats. Those criticisms are all the more pointed when the price of a single steak with a side of fries can equal the cost of a short tasting menu.

Accordingly, in this chapter you won't find classic steak houses whose clientele surely visit more on the basis of nostalgia than good culinary sensibilities. What makes eating red meat such a quintessentially New York experience isn't adherence to clubby traditions, but rather the sheer diversity of the city's offerings, including bandeja paisa platters at twenty-four-hour Colombian diners, elaborate tastings at Korean barbecue spots, smoked pastrami at Kosher delis, and Mexican barbacoa and adobada.

What follows is a list of the city's most quintessential chops, steaks, and other forms of red meat, most of them simply prepared and served with little adornment, save some salt, spices, or chiles.

Old Homestead
56 9th Avenue, Chelsea, Manhattan

The beef tastings at Cote:
New York is teeming with great Korean barbecue spots; what sets **Cote** (page 69) apart is its smart mash-up of K-town-style tabletop grilling and classic New York steak house fare.

Empanada Mama's bandeja paisa:
The traditional Colombian meat platter, which mixes Spanish and African sensibilities, easily works as a dinner for two at Empanada Mama in Hell's Kitchen (page 69) and is a heck of a deal. The cooks infuse skirt steak with so much juicy,

garlicky marinade, it practically bursts on the palate. Grilled chorizo, indented with a knife, boasts a nice smokiness and a toothsome chew. And chicharrons pack a gelatinous texture that recalls pork gummy bears. The dish also includes the requisite white rice, black beans, fried egg, sweet maduros, buttery arepa, and sliced avocado.

Guantanamera's vaca frita:

Guantanamera, a laid-back Hell's Kitchen hangout where Cuban singers croon from the small stage every night, will serve you a traditional strip steak if that's what you really want, but the smarter move is to sample a proper Caribbean specialty, like the thinly cut bistec de palomilla, or the classic vaca frita. Chefs slowly simmer a skirt steak, shred it, marinate it in mojo sauce, and then panfry it until it takes on the ropy texture of a tender beef jerky.

Guantanamera
939 8th Avenue, Hell's Kitchen, Manhattan

Prime rib at Smith & Wollensky:

Most prime ribs are straightforwardly beefy affairs; chefs slice the regal cut and pair it with jus and horseradish cream. But Smith & Wollensky on Third Avenue does things a bit differently, dry-aging the rib before seasoning it with enough

kosher salt to cause hypertension in a blue whale. The twenty-six-ounce roast boasts a pronounced Stilton funk on the spinalis dorsis (the fatty, brisket-like exterior), while the pink interior is leaner and cleaner.

Smith & Wollensky
797 3rd Avenue, Midtown East, Manhattan

Rib eye at Gallaghers:

Open since 1927, Gallaghers (page 70) ranks with—or perhaps just ahead of—Keens as the city's top old-school steak house, due in no small part to its house-dry-aged meats cooked over live wood coals. Your top choice here is the obscenely marbled rib eye, which is a solid cut for those who are new to the world of dry-aging. While certain steaks flaunt deep notes of blue cheese and minerality, this one is milder, giving off complex aromas of heady brown butter. The flesh itself, in turn, sports a pronounced sweetness, a silky tenderness, profound hits of beefiness when you bite into little morsels of fat, and a subtle hint of smoke from the majestic grill.

Gorgonzola-cured wagyu steak at Carne Mare:

This steak, at first glance, seems to sport the trappings of a stoner's midnight experiment. But chef Andrew Carmellini pulls off the feat at Carne Mare in the Seaport. The steak doesn't flaunt a funkiness that's necessarily more aggressive than other aged cuts; it's just that the gorgonzola tang is a bit clearer, without disappearing after a few bites. Yet, the nuances of the meat itself still shine, from the iron-y interior to the ultra-beefy exterior, which packs the greasy, griddle-style punch of a Shake Shack burger.

Carne Mare
89 South Street Seaport, Financial District, Manhattan

The mutton chop at Keens:

If most steak house cuts are somewhat neutral in their flavor profile, lamb packs more assertively grassy and funky notes, with a somewhat sweet flesh. More steak houses should serve them. Chef Bill Rodgers of Keens (page 71) uses a broiler to sear a two-pound saddle cut of year-old Colorado lamb, roasts it, then slathers it with mint-laced jus. This is lamb to the power of one

hundred, an essay in clean barnyard aromas, bloody tender meat, and musky fats.

Pastrami at Katz's or 2nd Ave Deli or Hometown:

The New York meat experience wouldn't be complete without pastrami—succulent beef that takes on a brick-red hue, with a signature pepper bark, following an elaborate cooking process that includes brining, sometimes boiling, spicing, smoking, and steaming. To help guide your eating, consider three different styles. At 2nd Ave Deli (page 85), the beef navel pastrami is thinly sliced and stacked high; it's so moist it reflects light. This is pastrami doing its best impression of prosciutto. At Katz's (page 36), by contrast, the counter workers slice the beef—also cut from the navel—to the ample thickness of Thanksgiving turkey, showing off the meat's smokiness with greater heft. And at Hometown Bar-B-Que (page 154), owner Billy Durney smokes and steams a brisket as marbled as wagyu; the fat is so ample, its sweetness actually manages to tame the meat's rampant salts.

Beef tongue and belly at Jongro Gopchang:

If you're looking for one of the city's most popular and accessible beef experiences, the famed Jongro Gopchang (page 70), a Korean barbecue spot, is a solid option, and a venue that's a heck of a lot easier to get into than Cote (page 69). Order anything, but it's one of the few beef-centric spots where one can find slightly fewer common cuts like belly, wonderfully marbled, or tongue; the latter cut sports a tremendously powerful bovine flavor. You grill the cuts tableside, seasoning them with salt and spicy and umami-rich ssamjang sauce.

Steak au poivre at Pastis and Corner Bar:

Two of the finest steaks au poivre in New York are so wildly different most patrons might not even classify them as being related. At Pastis in the Meatpacking District, chef Marjorie Meek-Bradley douses filet mignon in a creamy peppercorn sauce, enriching the lean meat with luscious dairy and gentle heat.

At Corner Bar (page 164), chefs Ignacio Mattos (Altro Paradiso and Estela, pages 12 and 36) and Jason Pfeifer take a Snake River Farms wagyu skirt and lay it atop a handsome, mahogany-hued au poivre. The charcoal-grilled meat packs a preternatural sweetness, while the sauce exudes a profound stickiness, a product of the fact that Pfeifer melts a wonderfully gelatinous calf's foot into the elixir. It is a study in obscene richness, cut only by a hint of red wine and occasional stings of peppery heat. At either venue, however, you finish the affair by dredging crisp fries through the indulgent sauces. Also worth checking out is the famed version at French classic Raoul's (page 15).

Pastis
52 Gansevoort Street, Meatpacking District, Manhattan

Butcher's cut at Le Marais:

New York has no shortage of kosher steak houses, but the French-bistro-themed Le Marais has long ranked near the top. The cooks here cut a darn good (and exceedingly tender) beef jerky, but for a main, the chief draw here is the butcher's cut, also known as the rib cap or spinalis dorsis. Rarely served by itself at a steak house, the rib cap packs a spider-like marbling with a pleasantly coarse, pull-apart, accordion-like texture. It is supremely beefy.

Le Marais
150 West 46th Street, Midtown West, Manhattan

Honey mustard duck at the Grill:
It's not uncommon to find an elegant slab of duck breast at any of the city's French or New American spots. Long Island and the Hudson Valley produce some of the country's finest birds—but the Grill (page 62), the restaurant that replaced Midtown icon the Four Seasons, does something a bit more majestic and steak-like. It doesn't pair the red-meat waterfowl with seasonal berries or greens, as is the norm, but rather plates it by itself: a slab of canard on a plate. And what a duck it is, sporting silky, medium-rare meat, a layer of fat that seems to dissolve like soft meringue, and a golden skin that shatters like crème brûlée. The honey mustard sauce, in turn, tames all the richness. This is duck pretending to be filet mignon, and it's a lot cheaper than the Grill's more expensive steaks.

Adobada at Los Tacos No. 1:
If you're in Times Square rushing to a movie or a show, you're in luck: Los Tacos has a location here as well as in Chelsea Market (page 14) and Tribeca, among others, and serves a strikingly delicious adobada taco. To make it they marinate thinly sliced pork shoulder in adobo sauce and cook it on a slowly rotating trompo. They slice off pieces, crisp them on the plancha, and pile on a corn tortilla with onions and a slice of pineapple. Add habanero salsa for heat, and there you have it, a gem of a pork taco delivered in mere minutes.

SPLURGES

New York is home to some of the country's most expensive restaurants, but not all of them are worth your limited funds. The modern Korean venues on page 52 and the following Manhattan standouts are all worth the splurge.

Aquavit
65 East 55th Street, Midtown East
This Michelin-starred Scandinavian restaurant (page 69) has been run by chef Emma Bengtsson since 2014 and is a fantastic power lunch option.

Carbone
181 Thompson Street, Greenwich Village
Diners come here (page 12) as much for the crowd-pleasing Italian red-sauce dishes as they do for the celebrity-spotting.

Eleven Madison Park
11 Madison Avenue, Flatiron
Go for the full vegan tasting menu at the restaurant (page 69), or try your luck as a walk-in at the bar for á la carte dishes and cocktails.

Gramercy Tavern
42 East 20th Street, Flatiron
Danny Meyer's warm and classic restaurant close to Union Square has maintained its status as a special-occasion destination for decades.

The Grill
99 East 52nd Street, Midtown East
The revamp of the New York City icon the Four Seasons is just as sophisticated as the original, but now the food is actually worth the expense.

Le Bernardin
155 West 51st Street, Midtown
This seafood temple (page 71), perfect for a celebratory meal, is still unparalleled when it comes to immaculate cooking and top-notch service.

Le Coucou
138 Lafayette Street, Little Italy
Here, chef Daniel Rose employs old-school techniques and serves French classics in one of the city's most gorgeous dining rooms.

Llama San
359 6th Avenue, West Village
This is a unique and high-end take on Japanese-Peruvian Nikkei cuisine.

Saga
70 Pine Street, 63rd floor, Financial District
It doesn't get more luxe than a multi-course meal at the top of a skyscraper. Come for the views; stay for James Kent's innovative American dishes.

Shuko
47 East 12th Street, Union Square
If you like your omakase paired with relaxed vibes, good music, and a killer wine list, try Shuko. It's less stuffy than other sushi places in town but still features true artistry from Masa and Neta vets Jummy Lau and Nick Kim.

Tempura Matsui
222 East 39th Street, Murray Hill
This one-of-a-kind tasting menu is focused only on the art of tempura.

SPOTLIGHT: STATEN ISLAND

Staten Island isn't on the radar of a lot of visitors to New York, but it boasts a quietly underrated food scene, packed with Italian American specialties, old European standbys, a growing number of Sri Lankan restaurants, and more.

Ayat Staten Island
2018 Hylan Boulevard, Midland Beach
This Palestinian fast-casual restaurant, which first opened in 2020 in Bay Ridge, has a location with a much larger dining room on Staten Island. Its sibling restaurant, Yemen Café (page 157), which also has multiple other locations, is nearby. Both are great for halal Staten Island options.

Denino's
524 Port Richmond Avenue, Port Richmond
Denino's is the first name in Staten Island pizza, and its clam pie, otherwise hard to find in the city, is the move.

Egger's Ice Cream Parlor
Multiple locations
Scoops of nostalgia are on the menu at this old-fashioned ice cream parlor from circa the 1930s (in its current location since the 1950s).

Flagship Brewing Co.
40 Minthorne Street, Tompkinsville
Swing by Staten Island's homegrown craft brewery for a pint at the taproom. Then, pick up a few four- or six-packs to take home, plus merch to commemorate your visit to the "forgotten borough," as the locals sometimes call it.

Killmeyer's
4254 Arthur Kill Road, Charleston
Decades-old German restaurant Killmeyer's is ideal for a hearty meal of Wiener schnitzel and German sausages, with a requisite pint in hand.

Lakruwana
668 Bay Street, Stapleton Heights
This Sri Lankan restaurant is a can't-miss, not only because it serves one of the city's last remaining all-you-can-eat deals, but also because it's one of the island's most ornately decorated restaurants, with antiques in every corner. Look out for their weekend all-you-can-eat buffets, which offer abundant options in ornate clay vessels (see below).

Lee's Tavern
60 Hancock Street, Dongan Hills
If you're in the mood for thin-crust bar-style pizza pie, you can't do better than Lee's Tavern, open since the 1940s.

Sandwich and Pickle
1949 Richmond Avenue, Bullshead
This newfangled modern delicatessen serves matzo ball soup, pickle platters, Reuben eggs Benedict, and other Jewish-leaning dishes that make you feel like you're back in Bubby's living room.

Hell's Kitchen
Herald Square
Kips Bay
Koreatown
Midtown East
Midtown West
Murray Hill
Nomad
Rockefeller Center
Times Square

MIDT
& FLAT

3

OWN IRON

MIDTOWN & FLATIRON

DINING

1. Aquavit
2. Atomix
3. Burger Joint
4. Café China
5. Cote
6. Donburiya
7. Eleven Madison Park
8. Empanada Mama
9. Gallaghers Steakhouse
10. Grand Central Oyster Bar
11. The Halal Guys
12. Indian Accent
13. Jongro Gopchang
14. Kang Ho Dong Baekjeong
15. Keens Steakhouse
16. Kjun
17. Koloman
18. Le Bernardin
19. Le Rock
20. Lodi
21. Marea
22. Margon
23. Milu
24. P.J. Clarke's
25. Pocha 32
26. S&P Lunch
27. Three Roosters
28. Victor's Café
29. Yakitori Torishin

SHOPPING

1. Fishs Eddy
2. Grand Central Market
3. J. B. Prince Company
4. Kalustyan's
5. Katagiri Japanese Grocery
6. Kreuther Handcrafted Chocolate
7. La Boîte
8. MoMA Design Store

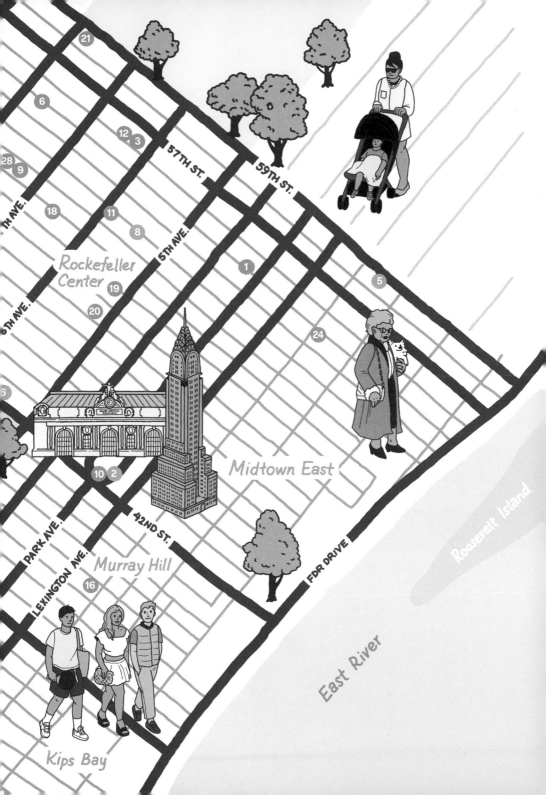

57TH ST.

59TH ST.

28
9

6

21

12
3

18

11

8

Rockefeller
Center

19

20

5TH AVE.

6TH AVE.

1

5

24

Midtown East

10
2

42ND ST.

PARK AVE.

LEXINGTON AVE.

Murray Hill

16

Kips Bay

FDR DRIVE

Roosevelt Island

East River

MIDTOWN & FLATIRON
DINING

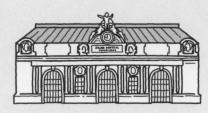

Midtown is sort of the postcard that most tourists have in their mind when they think of Manhattan: luminescent Times Square (doubling as the spot where the ball drops each New Year's), the sparkling Broadway marquees, entertainment centers like Madison Square Garden, museums like the Museum of Modern Art, ice-skating and *Saturday Night Live* at Rockefeller Center, and those iconic lions on the New York Public Library steps.

To most locals, however, Midtown is a place to pass through. A major transit hub for buses coming into the Port Authority and trains at Penn Station and Grand Central, Midtown is nothing if not crowded with people coming and going. Back in the 1970s, before Times Square became the light-filled, overstimulating attraction that it is today, the area was seedier, the headquarters for sex shops and other vices. Over the past couple of decades, though, Midtown has been better known as an office worker–friendly food neighborhood—with either spots that cater to quick service for on-the-go bites or more lavish, spendy restaurants for power lunches or after-work splurges.

Overall, though, Midtown is centrally located and where almost every subway line connects. Once a more working-class area, Midtown is being encroached on by what's known as the Billionaires' Row—jaw-droppingly expensive apartments for the 1 percent—just a stone's throw away from the glitzy mall Hudson Yards, with its high-end restaurants and chain clothing stores. Though Midtown can be swamped with newcomers to New York, with this book we can help you act like a local and find some of those hidden gems that still make coming to this area worth it. Use this chapter as a guide to dining before and after Broadway shows, depending on how far you're willing to travel. If you're eating before, don't be shy about giving your server a heads-up that you have a show to catch—any restaurant in the vicinity of the Theater District will have lots of experience getting diners out quickly. Plus we offer guidance on the ever-rewarding micro-neighborhood of Koreatown and the oft-overlooked office-worker center of Flatiron.

For our purposes here, we're including restaurants between Twenty-Third Street and Central Park South, east of Fifth Avenue (to include Flatiron), and Thirtieth to Fifty-Ninth west of Fifth Avenue.

1. Aquavit
65 East 55th Street,
Midtown East

This esteemed Scandinavian restaurant went through an overhaul in 2019, making the fine-dining restaurant feel a bit more updated and casual than it originally was—though prices are still more special occasion here. In the main dining room, there are tasting menus, but you can have a more pick-your-own adventure at the bar. Definitely order the princess cake: a delicious blue dome of raspberry, whipped cream, and marzipan.

2. Atomix
104 East 30th Street,
Kips Bay

This restaurant from the team behind the small-plates-focused Atoboy showcases how fine dining can truly be an art form. The Korean tasting-menu spot offers plating that's as creative as the set of ten note cards—featuring minimalist visual representations of the dishes—that come with each meal and are worthy of being framed.

3. Burger Joint
119 West 56th Street,
Midtown West

Burger Joint, hidden behind a curtain in a posh Midtown hotel lobby, is meant to be a bit of a secret, but the lines give it away. It serves low-key one of the best burgers in town. The interiors are made to look like a dive bar with graffiti and stickers collaged on the walls and a Ferris Bueller poster you'd find in a teenager's bedroom.

4. Café China
59 West 37th Street,
Herald Square

Café China is a rare Midtown restaurant that genuinely feels cool. The Sichuan food is incredible, but the interior design is really what sets it apart from its competitors: No detail is spared here, with mood lighting, jade-green tables, vintage mirrors, and porcelain servingware.

5. Cote
16 West 22nd Street,
Flatiron

Cote combines the traditional high-end steak house experience—premium cuts of beef, wedge salads, and shrimp cocktail—with the flavors, vibes, and dynamism of Korean barbecue. Whether you keep it simple with the more budget-friendly set menu or opt for reserve cuts, steak tartare with caviar, and rare wine, it makes for an extremely fun and decadent night. The restaurant is so popular it spawned a Miami sibling, as well as Coqodaq, a fried chicken spot.

6. Donburiya
253 West 55th Street,
Hell's Kitchen

Long known to be a destination the service industry hits up after clocking out, Donburiya has a lengthy izakaya menu filled with rice bowls with eel or pork katsu, ramen, and more.

7. Eleven Madison Park
11 Madison Avenue,
Flatiron

In 2021, Eleven Madison Park shocked longtime followers by announcing it would convert to an all-vegan menu. Regardless of whether you eat meat, if you're looking to feel like a major baller and want to see what one of the most acclaimed chefs in the world can do without animal products, this could be worth a visit. Just note it remains one of the hardest reservations in town.

8. Empanada Mama
765 9th Avenue,
Hell's Kitchen

It is increasingly hard to find restaurants that are open twenty-four hours a day, but Empanada Mama—which specializes in wheat or corn flour empanadas with fillings like curried chicken, ham and pineapple, and Colombian-style beef with corn—fills that late-night void. A tasty, affordable option before or after seeing a Broadway musical, or in the wee hours when you need sustenance to sop up booze, it's a wild scene where people come after clubbing or getting off work.

9. Gallaghers Steakhouse
228 West 52nd Street,
Times Square

Another classic steak house in New York, the decades-old Gallaghers is a favorite among theatergoers. Gallaghers is beloved for its old-timey vibe, but it also goes the extra mile to dry-age the beef in-house and cook it over a charcoal grill. The prime rib—with bountiful jus and horseradish cream—is so popular it's often sold out. Call in your order that morning to lock in a taste of one of the city's most elusive dishes.

10. Grand Central Oyster Bar
89 East 42nd Street
Midtown East

Since 1913, the historic and grandiose Grand Central Terminal has welcomed travelers from near and far—and so has the Grand Central Oyster Bar. The cavernous tiled architecture and red-and-white

checkerboard tablecloths make it one of those touristy New York things that's actually still a lot of fun. Sit back with a plate of fresh oysters and a martini in hand before hopping on the train to your next stop.

11. The Halal Guys
6th Avenue and West 53rd Street,
Midtown West

The Halal Guys is easily one of the most famous food carts in NYC, save for maybe the hot dog stands littering Midtown. In 1990 the three Egyptian founders started their business as a hot dog stand, eventually moving on to sell their now-famous falafel platters and chicken over rice (shown below) to Muslim cabdrivers, who back then couldn't find halal food as easily. These days, the carts have spread all over the city, and people with or without dietary restrictions head here for their filling platters.

12. Indian Accent
123 West 56th Street,
Midtown West

Considered to be one of the best Indian restaurants in New York City, Indian Accent serves a menu of classics with inventive, well, accents, inspired by global cooking and luxury ingredients. You'll want to dress up a bit here and make a reservation in advance.

13. Jongro Gopchang
22 West 32nd Street, 5th floor,
Koreatown

Jongro BBQ, a chain restaurant from Seoul, serves excellent Korean barbecue. But its sister restaurant next door, known for its gopchang, or intestines, is also something to behold. There's a sort of musical quality to being at this Koreatown classic, where meat—standard cuts in addition to the offal—sizzles at the center of the table on cast-iron grills.

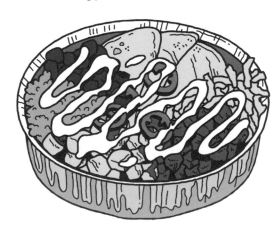

14. Kang Ho Dong Baekjeong
1 East 32nd Street, Koreatown

An outpost of a popular Korean chain that first arrived in Los Angeles, Kang Ho Dong Baekjeong has become an essential Korean barbecue spot in Koreatown, with long wait times during prime-time dinner hours to match. Known for its interactive tableside grills, you can sizzle up one of their high-quality cuts of meat that range from beef to pork as well as eggs and veggies.

15. Keens Steakhouse
72 West 36th Street, Herald Square

Even if you don't love steak houses, Keens is undeniably fun and an important part of New York history, open since 1885 and a favorite among dignitaries and locals alike. This New York icon has walls covered with vintage mismatched memorabilia, including what's considered to be one of the world's largest collections of smoking pipes, in a space that is casual but celebratory, and a favorite for birthdays. Stick to the classics here: Start with a shrimp cocktail, then steak and French fries are the move, or consider the mutton chop (page 59).

16. Kjun
154 East 39th Street, Murray Hill

Korean meets New Orleans at this Murray Hill hot spot that started as a pop-up with dishes like fried chicken, tomato kimchi, and jambalaya, or shrimp and grits in shrimp dashi. Now the menu is a robust collection of snacks, sides, and hearty meat dishes served in a warm but casual dining area.

17. Koloman
16 West 29th Street, Nomad

Koloman, an Austrian restaurant just off the lobby of Nomad's Ace Hotel, serves a full Viennese breakfast by day. By night, chef Markus Glocker highlights modern, fanciful interpretations of the cuisine in the form of dishes like a celery root tartare and beet linzer, with lübeck marzipan and a souffle to share for dessert.

18. Le Bernardin
155 West 51st Street, Midtown West

If there's one restaurant in Midtown that's worth prices as sky-high as the buildings, it's Le Bernardin. Eric Ripert's palace to all things seafood is a serene spot for a power lunch or a special dinner date. Le Bernardin does several versions of tasting menus—it's as fine dining as dining in New York really gets—serving the most pristine seafood meal you'll ever have (with options for vegetarians too).

19. Le Rock
45 Rockefeller Plaza, Rockefeller Center

Developers hoping to revitalize the tired and touristy Rockefeller Center invited some of the city's hippest restaurateurs to open outposts throughout the complex in 2022. Le Rock, a high-end French restaurant with natural wine and downtown vibes, from the team behind Tribeca's Frenchette (page 13), has done the best job so far making a case for the development. Book in advance and brace for chaos, especially if you want to visit while the tree is up right outside.

20. Lodi

1 Rockefeller Plaza,
Rockefeller Center

Just when power lunches felt like a relic of the *Mad Men* era, Ignacio Mattos (behind Altro Paradiso and Estela, pages 12 and 36) opened a high-end lunch spot in the recently revitalized Rockefeller Plaza. The menu leans Italian, with lots of antipasti, salumi, and cheese.

21. Marea

240 Central Park South,
Midtown West

If you're dining on someone else's expense account, make a beeline to Marea. One of the top spots in the city for both seafood and pasta, even after all these years, Marea lands the jump with octopus fusilli, gnocchetti with shrimp, and other al dente delights.

22. Margon

136 West 46th Street,
Times Square

On weekdays, all types of workers line up at this tiny counter spot to order one thing and one thing alone: Cuban sandwiches. Margon is definitely no secret to those who work in the area, but as long as you don't go during lunch rush, this is a can't-skip casual Midtown eat.

23. Milu

333 Park Avenue South,
Flatiron

This fast-casual restaurant is a favorite among office workers looking for a more exciting affordable lunch than a Sweetgreen. That's because this Chinese restaurant comes from Eleven Madison Park alum Connie Chung, and she brings her expertise to chile crisp chicken bowls, mandarin duck, and egg tart soft serve.

24. P.J. Clarke's

915 3rd Avenue,
Midtown East

This pub has been open since 1884 and has since sprouted several locations throughout the city, but the original Midtown building really does give a taste of New York. In its heyday, P.J. Clarke's was a regular celebrity hangout, but now it's a go-to for work happy hours, local families, and anyone seeking out a solid burger and a beer.

25. Pocha 32

15 West 32nd Street, 2nd floor,
Koreatown

Koreatown is easily one of the best neighborhoods in New York for going out. Korean barbecue joints take advantage of late-night hours to service partiers and karaoke denizens. Pocha 32 is a bar that stays open until three A.M. on weekends and where people tend to order the budae jjigae—the spicy kimchi stew—while sloshing back soju.

26. S&P Lunch

174 5th Avenue,
Flatiron

When Flatiron luncheonette Eisenberg's closed, New Yorkers mourned the loss. Thankfully, the team behind Court Street Grocers (page 153) reopened the space as S&P Lunch (a nod to the space's original name, S&P Sandwich) and left the old-school digs intact. Wait times can be long for the swivel-stool and booth seating, but the egg cream, the Jersey Joe with Russian dressing, the carrot cake, and the matzo ball bowl soup are more than worth it. There are few spots that feel as both new-and-old New York as this.

27. Three Roosters

792 9th Avenue,
Hell's Kitchen

It can be hell to find the right lunch spot in Hell's Kitchen, but fear not at the fast-casual Three Roosters. Rather than opening a Thai restaurant with the take-out staples more common in New York such as pad Thai, Three Roosters is about chicken—slippery cuts of white meat—served grilled, poached, or fried over rice with sliced cucumbers and various sweet and spicy sauces.

28. Victor's Café
236 West 52nd Street,
Times Square

Harder to find than dinner in Midtown is an ideal brunch spot. Victor's Café should be on your list for its excellent serving of ropa vieja, the national dish of Cuba. Originally opened on the Upper West Side in the 1960s, two decades later it relocated to its current location near Times Square and is still serving up Cuban favorites.

29. Yakitori Torishin
362 West 53rd Street,
Hell's Kitchen

Torishin is a shrine to chicken, which the skilled chefs grill on skewers over charcoal flames behind a large wraparound counter. The meal here, which can be à la carte or ordered as a set or an omakase, is a parade of chicken parts, including nuggets of crunchy knee bone (yes, eat it), succulent thighs, crispy wings, and a meatball with a side of egg yolk to dip it in. They do wonders with vegetables and other meats, but chicken is the star here.

QR CODES for our online guides to **MIDTOWN & FLATIRON** neighborhoods:

FLATIRON

HELL'S KITCHEN

MIDTOWN EAST

PENN STATION

THEATER DISTRICT

TIMES SQUARE

MIDTOWN AND FLATIRON
SHOPPING

Home to the city's biggest transportation hubs and the centers for business that house many commuters from nine to five, the area also vibrates with a businesslike seriousness, the spectacle of Times Square notwithstanding. But for the shopper passionate about food and dining, there are still worthy destinations. A concentration of Japanese restaurants and shops brings an international flair to the neighborhood, though these tend to be more upscale than those farther south in the East Village's Little Tokyo. And that same air of professionalism has given rise to best-in-class shops that cater to pros in the culinary field as well as the refined epicures.

1. Fishs Eddy
889 Broadway,
Flatiron

For more than three decades Fishs Eddy (named for a hamlet upstate) has been affordably—and cheekily—stocking kitchen cabinets. While you'll find other kitchen accessories, such as dish towels and utensils, dishes are the star here, lining the walls and in stacks on carts, tables, and shelving throughout the sizable space. Among these, there are options for floral motifs or diner-style stripes, along with a heavy helping of kitsch and New York City iconography of the ilk that's as likely to be a souvenir carried out of state as it is to appear on the breakfast table of an actual New Yorker.

2. Grand Central Market
89 East 42nd Street,
Midtown East

On the main level of New York's most famous train station, a narrow passageway houses some of the city's most emblematic food vendors, including outposts of Li-Lac Chocolates, Zabar's (page 91), Murray's Cheese (page 18), and Brooklyn bakery Bien Cuit. It's the most convenient place to pick up a snack or host gift on your way to Westchester or the Hudson Valley.

3. J. B. Prince Company
36 East 31st Street, 6th floor,
Nomad

Anyone who's ever wondered where ice sculptors buy their carving saws should pencil in a stop at J. B. Prince. This is where professionals head for the tools of the trade. Knives, cookware, and commercial-level tools are displayed on utilitarian racks on the sixth floor of a Midtown office building, a location that makes it especially clear that it's a store for those most in the know. But if you need a piece of equipment, whether a vacuum sealer or pair of plating tweezers, there's nowhere better.

4. Kalustyan's
123 Lexington Avenue,
Kips Bay

Originally a specialty store for Indian spices and groceries, Kalustyan's has since grown to become the go-to of chefs and home cooks alike for ingredients from the world over. If a cookbook requests an obscure spice or particular variety of rice, odds are you'll find it at Kalustyan's. For the sake of your time, it's perhaps best to go in with some idea of what you're looking for, or you'll likely lose track of time marveling at racks upon racks of spices, legumes, and condiments, and trays of tempting jalebis and Turkish delight.

5. Katagiri Japanese Grocery
224 East 59th Street,
Midtown East

At more than a century old, Katagiri is the oldest Japanese grocery store in the United States. And while its place in history might be reason enough to pay it a visit, the jam-packed snack aisle is a better one. When you've finished loading your cart with Pocky and potato sticks, you can turn your attention to the non-edible, such as basic Japanese cooking tools (think matcha whisks and bamboo sushi mats) or cutesy food-shaped erasers.

6. Kreuther Handcrafted Chocolate

41 West 42nd Street, Midtown West

Located just next door to his eponymous fine dining restaurant, Kreuther Handcrafted Chocolate is Alsatian chef Gabriel Kreuther's luxe love letter to chocolate. Here, visitors can watch as chocolatiers, led by pastry chef Marc Aumont, craft bonbons, ganaches, and other chocolate confections.

7. La Boîte

724 11th Avenue, Hell's Kitchen

La Boîte launched as a biscuit company, but when owner Lior Lev Sercarz opened a brick-and-mortar, it was with the primary purpose of selling spices, both single varieties and his own blends, at times in partnership with chefs like Eric Ripert. The biscuits, however, are still available in a giftable tin. Here, too, owner Sercarz's passion for spices is clear in flavors like hawayej, dates, and orange and zuta, mint, and almond.

8. MoMA Design Store

44 West 53rd Street, Midtown West

With two locations and a robust e-commerce operation, the MoMA Design Store is far more than your typical museum gift shop. Here, as at a downtown location in Soho, you can browse iconic pieces of modern design, such as the Alessi bird-whistle teakettle or MoMA's own satellite bowl, and peruse all the kitchen tools and tableware destined to be future museum-worthy design pieces.

BEYOND RESTAURANTS

Coffee Shops
Bibble & Sip
Culture Espresso
Gumption Coffee
Little Collins
Ralph's Coffee

Bars
Aldo Sohm Wine Bar
Ardesia Wine Bar
The Campbell
Jimmy's Corner
The bar at Keens
The Rum House

Bakeries
Amy's Bread
Bien Cuit
Bourke Street Bakery
Bread Story
Breads Bakery
Dominique Ansel
    Workshop

Ice Cream
Caffè Panna
Davey's Ice Cream
Soft Swerve

Food Halls
Mercado Little Spain
Urban Hawker

NYC FOOD GLOSSARY

By Robert Sietsema

Appetizing store: Though few appetizing stores still exist, the concept is unique to New York City's Ashkenazi Jewish community and first appeared likely sometime in the 1800s. Spots like Russ & Daughters (page 44), Zabar's (page 91), Barney Greengrass (page 85), or Simply Nova sell smoked fish like cut-to-order gravlax and other provisions.

Baked pretzels: In New York, the soft pretzel is as ubiquitous a street food as SpongeBob ice cream Popsicles and hot dogs. Usually, they're covered with big, coarse salt and eaten as is on the go.

Bialy: New Yorkers who love to boast that their bagels are the best are the same folks who have opinions on where to get the biggest, freshest, and best-tasting ones. But overlooked in this debate is the bialy, a flat, round roll with onions chopped up in the center, originating in the town of Białystok, Poland. Ask for one of those in a bagel store or deli (or a bialy bakery like Kossar's) and receive an admiring nod of the head from the proprietor.

Black and white: This archetypal term refers to an ancient kind of cookie—more like a flattish cake—that has white frosting on one side and black frosting on the other, with the line separating them perfectly bisecting the circle. It may have originally been created as a tribute to Henry Hudson's ship the *Half Moon*.

Bodega: In most parts of the country, it's called a convenience store, 7-Eleven, or, if you happen to live in San Antonio, an ice house. Here, that type of small corner store (and nearly every block in some parts of the city has one) is called a bodega. It's where New Yorkers get everything from their morning coffee to beer to toiletries, and their favorite bacon, egg, and cheese (see pages 92–97).

Celery soda: Often sold at Jewish delicatessens in the city and newer sandwich shops going for a retro feel, this soda is often likened to ginger ale but has a much more vegetal, savory essence to it. It first appeared in New York City sometime around the 1860s from local soda brand Dr. Brown's, still popular in the city today. Slurp it down with a pastrami sandwich, preferably with a pickle on the side.

Chopped cheese: Also known as chop cheese, this is a greasy, delightful mixture of ground beef burger chopped up and mixed with onions and slices of American cheese. In New York, one of the best versions of the chopped cheese sandwich has long been found at East Harlem's Blue Sky Deli, formerly known as Hajji's—but the concoction has also taken on new life in empanadas, burritos, and sliders.

Cuchifritos: Cuchifritos are a Puerto Rican snack staple generally made of fried pork. Though restaurants all over the five boroughs prepare them, one of its more famous examples is the namesake 188 Bakery Cuchifritos in the Bronx (page 98), which had a cameo in Anthony Bourdain's *Parts Unknown*.

Dimes Square: A made-up nickname for the micro-neighborhood where the Lower East Side meets Chinatown at East Broadway, where the perennially hip, healthy sibling restaurants called Dimes and Dimes Deli reside. Insiders use the neighborhood's name as a quasi-inside joke to reference the scene—which includes ultra-hip restaurants like Cervo's (page 35),

dive bar Clandestino, wine bar Le Dive, Greek restaurant Kiki's (page 37), the Metrograph movie theater and its upstairs restaurant, as well as the Nine Orchard hotel property (page 164)—which is especially good for people-watching downtown New York fashion kids.

Doubles: This term, which is both singular and plural, refers to a marvelous small sandwich made with a pair of tiny puri stuffed with curried chickpeas (called "chana"), topped with two sauces, one fiery, one fruity. It originated in Trinidad among those of Indian descent and now is a favorite snack in parts of Brooklyn, Queens, and the Bronx.

Egg cream: Oddly, this signature beverage of New York City—which is getting harder to find all the time—contains no eggs and no cream. Rather, it's a shot of chocolate or vanilla syrup (Fox's U-Bet is the local brand) mixed with milk and club soda, with the proportion of ingredients and stirring style unique to each maker.

Halal cart: A halal cart is a food truck in New York that serves dishes like chicken over rice, shawarma, and other halal-friendly staples, parked all over NYC, especially around Midtown. A true halal cart is affordable (usually cash only), and the food comes boxed up in Styrofoam or tinfoil containers. They've become a staple in NYC's food truck scene, helped along by the popularity of the Halal Guys (page 70) food cart (now a nationwide chain) over the past two decades, which went from mainly servicing Muslim taxicab drivers looking for a rare halal option to appearing on nearly every street corner in Midtown.

New York–style cheesecake: New York–style cheesecake differs from regular cheesecake by going heavy on cream cheese, rather than heavy cream, in its recipes. It's thought to have been originated in the 1920s by the owner of the now defunct Reuben's Restaurant and Delicatessen in Manhattan, but in the 1950s, the world-famous Junior's really staked a claim on the dish, helping make it a household name for New Yorkers.

Pastrami: Pastrami appeared in New York in the nineteenth century from Romanian immigrants: The cured and smoked beef brisket has become a New York icon at Jewish delicatessens around the city, especially Katz's Delicatessen (page 36), where the pastrami sandwich, usually on seedy rye bread with a pickle or coleslaw on the side, reigns supreme.

Rice rolls: Rice rolls, also known as cheung fun, are a breakfast street food made from thick rice noodles (with fillings like pork, shrimp, or veggies) that hails from the Guangdong province of China. Over the past five years, the Cantonese dish has increased its presence in New York City in Flushing at the original location of popular Joe's Steam Rice Roll, as well as in Manhattan's Chinatown, where you can find them at daytime street carts, rice roll counter restaurants, and dim sum establishments.

Schmear: When ordering a bagel, asking for a schmear ("just a little") is the way to get just the right amount of cream cheese.

Spumoni: An Italian American summer treat, spumoni ice cream is tricolored like the Italian flag. It veers from Neapolitan—which often is stripes of vanilla, strawberry, and chocolate ice cream—instead offering swirling pistachio, cherry, and vanilla. Though the spumoni ice cream wasn't invented in New York, we've claimed it as our own at L&B Spumoni Gardens (page 154), the pizzeria famous as much for its grandma-style pies as the dessert.

East Harlem
Fort George
Harlem
Lincoln Square
Morningside Heights
Upper East Side
Upper West Side
Washington Heights

UPTO

4

OWN

UPTOWN

DINING

1. 2nd Ave Deli
2. Africa Kine
3. Atlas Kitchen
4. Bánh
5. Barney Greengrass
6. Bombay Frankie Roti Roll
7. Calle 191 Pescaderia
8. Charles Pan-Fried Chicken
9. Gray's Papaya
10. H&H Bagels
11. Izzy's Smokehouse
12. Jacob's Pickles
13. JG Melon
14. Jing Fong
15. Lexington Candy Shop
16. Malecon
17. The Migrant Kitchen
18. Mission Ceviche
19. Native Noodles
20. Red Rooster
21. Schaller & Weber
22. Sushi Noz
23. Sylvia's
24. Taqueria 86
25. Tatiana by Kwame Onwuachi
26. Teranga
27. Tom's Restaurant

SHOPPING

1. Harlem Chocolate Factory
2. Kee's Chocolates
3. Kitchen Arts & Letters
4. Mondel Chocolates
5. William Greenberg Desserts
6. Zabar's

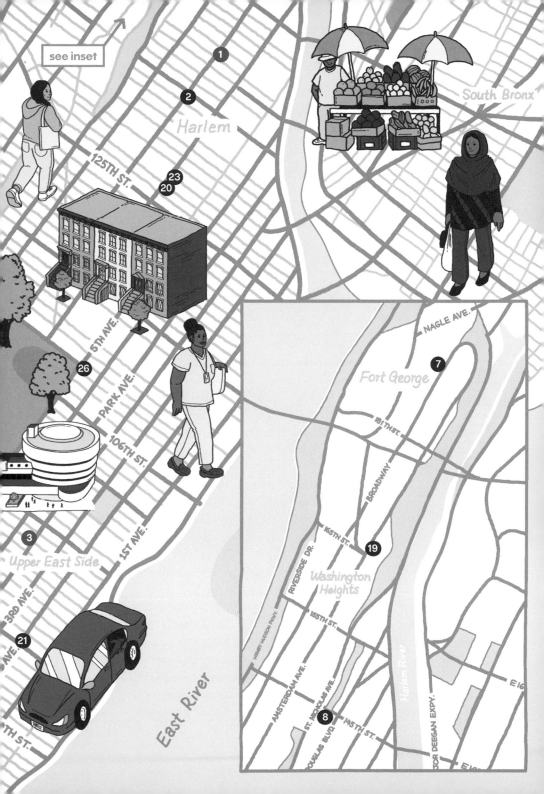

see inset

UPTOWN
DINING

To some New Yorkers, the Upper East and West Sides might as well be the suburbs. There's an extraordinary amount of wealth centralized in these residential areas—home to bankers, celebrities, and politicians—and yet they're considered some of the sleepiest dining scenes. Where uptown has always excelled is in its bagels and Jewish delicatessens—not to mention a slew of bougier fine-dining establishments for special occasions.

In recent years, that reputation has shifted slightly, which means there's more than just pricey meals to be had. After checking out Museum Mile—on the east side, a stretch of Manhattan that has dozens of museums, like the Metropolitan Museum of Art and the Guggenheim (and on the west side, the American Museum of Natural History)—these days you can taste Vietnamese, Sichuan, Nigerian, and Mexican food, too. One of the best reasons to come up this far north is, of course, the sprawling fields of Central Park—there's plenty of food nearby for picnics.

Farther north are Columbia University and the restaurants that cater to a student population. Harlem remains a leader in soul food in New York, with classics like Sylvia's, as well as newcomers, and one of the most vital dining neighborhoods in the city, which you don't want to skip, especially after a show at the storied Apollo Theater. Meanwhile, even farther north, Washington Heights and Inwood, more mountainous and neighborhood-y areas, have a dizzying array of cuisines to offer, particularly great for inexpensive dining options.

1. 2nd Ave Deli
1442 1st Avenue,
Upper East Side

After decades at its Second Avenue location in the East Village, this historic institution closed its doors in the early aughts and relocated to Midtown East and later the Upper East Side. They're known for blintzes, borscht, and other certified kosher Jewish staples. Upstairs at the Upper East Side outpost, there's a cocktail bar called 2nd Floor Bar & Essen.

2. Africa Kine
2267 Adam Clayton Powell Jr. Boulevard, Harlem

A Harlem restaurant with a strong local following, Africa Kine serves up some of the best West African food in the borough, including lamb curry, mafe (lamb or chicken in peanut sauce) with splatterings of red palm oil, and thiebu djen (stuffed fish and vegetables over rice).

3. Atlas Kitchen
258 West 109th Street,
Morningside Heights

Located conveniently near Columbia University, Atlas Kitchen is a favorite among students. The restaurant is what Eater NY critic Robert Sietsema calls "a culinary tour of China," with nods to Hunan and Sichuan provinces. The contemporary menu highlights dishes like crispy pork intestines, rice noodle soup with spicy pig trotters, and shredded potato with salted egg yolk. The sleek, gallery-like dining room is a nice respite from a day trapezing the city.

4. Bánh
942 Amsterdam Avenue,
Upper West Side

The Upper West Side isn't known for great Vietnamese restaurants, but Bánh is building a new legacy—it's easily one of the coolest restaurants to open in the area in the past ten years. The restaurant comes from Nhu Ton and John Nguyen, behind Cơm Tấm Ninh Kiều in the Bronx. The bún chả—a barbecue platter with vermicelli noodles—is popular, as are the crispy rice cakes with ground pork and mung bean filling that come with a sweet soy dressing.

5. Barney Greengrass
541 Amsterdam Avenue,
Upper West Side

A neighborhood delicatessen and appetizing store, Barney Greengrass looks largely untouched from when it first opened in 1908. People of all ages collide here over bagels with lox, sable, pastrami-spiced cuts of salmon, and crispy potato latkes served with sour cream and apple sauce (shown above).

6. Bombay Frankie Roti Roll
994 Amsterdam Avenue,
Upper West Side

Bombay frankies, a name for the street food of Mumbai, are on the menu at this narrow fast-casual Upper West Side stall. Rolled-up, portable rotis come stuffed with fillings like pickled paneer, tofu mushroom, and a masala omelet.

7. Calle 191 Pescaderia
1609 St. Nicholas Avenue,
Fort George
Just north of Washington Heights, this Dominican establishment handily combines a fish market with a restaurant. The space is decorated with artificial palm trees, and the lengthy menu features nearly every Spanish and Latin Caribbean seafood dish imaginable. One favorite is the marvelous asopao de camarones, a tomato-and-vinegar rice soup flavored with garlic and cilantro, generously dotted with large shrimp.

8. Charles Pan-Fried Chicken
340 West 145th Street,
Harlem
As the name suggests, chef and James Beard semifinalist Charles Gabriel—a household name in the area—takes the painstaking effort of preparing his fried chicken in a skillet. Now on an expansion tear throughout uptown Manhattan, Gabriel's new fast-casual restaurants keep that poultry as perfectly crisp as ever, with several other locations in Harlem and on the Upper West Side.

9. Gray's Papaya
2090 Broadway,
Upper West Side
This hot dog New York classic remains open at all hours of the day, and it's a tourist trap that's actually worth it. Plus, two franks and a medium drink for $6.95 is an especially unbeatable deal.

10. H&H Bagels
526 Columbus Avenue,
Upper West Side
Hot bagels and quick service are the name of the game here. This bagel shop—with several locations throughout the city, including one on the Upper East Side—has been making those legendary circles since 1972.

11. Izzy's Smokehouse
660 Amsterdam Avenue,
Upper West Side
Considered to be the city's first kosher Texas-style smokehouse, Izzy's first opened in Crown Heights in 2015 and now has an outpost on the Upper West Side. The brisket sandwich is the move here.

12. Jacob's Pickles
509 Amsterdam Avenue,
Upper West Side
This Upper West Side favorite blends Southern bites with Jewish inflections for an overall menu that's as comforting as can be. There's deviled eggs, biscuit sandwiches, matzo ball soup, and, of course, pickles.

13. JG Melon
1291 3rd Avenue,
Upper East Side
The glowing red sign of the Upper East Side stalwart beckons guests from near and far for one

thing: burgers. JG Melon is considered citywide to have some of the best burgers, but it's the vibe that makes it stand the test of time. First opened in 1972, this cash-only restaurant has a retro, taverny feel, with its green-and-white checkerboard tablecloth, jukebox, and vintage melon-themed objects hidden around the restaurant like a game of "I Spy."

14. Jing Fong
**380 Amsterdam Avenue,
Upper West Side**
In an area where dim sum can otherwise be hard to come by, Chinatown favorite Jing Fong has an outpost serving all of its family-style classics—har gow dumplings, shrimp-and-pork turnip cakes, scallion pancakes—just a few blocks from the American Museum of Natural History. Pile your table high with the steamed baskets and take home leftovers to nosh on late at night in your hotel room.

15. Lexington Candy Shop
**1226 Lexington Avenue,
Upper East Side**
Located just a stone's throw from the Metropolitan Museum of Art, this old-school luncheonette serves up plenty of diner classics with a dose of nostalgia. Don't miss out on the must-order egg cream, a sundae, or a root beer float.

16. Malecon
**4141 Broadway,
Washington Heights**
This Dominican Caribbean restaurant, with locations on the Upper West Side and Washington Heights, has roots in the area's Latin American community. Expect quick-and-easy service in a casual atmosphere. The restaurant calls itself the "king of roast chicken," and while that might be debatable, there's an extensive list of poultry served sauteed with garlic sauce, a la plancha (grilled), or simmering in a creamy shrimp sauce.

17. The Migrant Kitchen
**157 Columbus Avenue,
Lincoln Square**
The Migrant Kitchen is a fast-casual restaurant influenced by the fusing of dishes from immigrants in New York City. Its Lincoln Center–adjacent operation is its flagship, and here you'll find lunch items like cauliflower shawarma with pickled turnips, chicken tinga empanadas, and a sumac-Aleppo-roasted lamb torta. There are several other locations, including one in Central Park.

18. Mission Ceviche
**1400 2nd Avenue,
Upper East Side**
Mission Ceviche specializes in the tart and punchy raw fish dish of ceviche. What began as a food hall stall has since blossomed into its first full-service Peruvian joint on the Upper East Side. In a neighborhood with lots of pricey European restaurants, Mission offers a taste out of the ordinary.

BEYOND RESTAURANTS

Coffee Shops
Birch Coffee
Hutch and Waldo
Maman
Variety Coffee
 Roasters

Bars
Bemelmans Bar
The Dead Poet
Nobody Told Me

Bakeries
Egidio Pastry Shop
The Hungarian Pastry
 Shop
Lee Lee's Baked Goods
Levain Bakery
Madonia Bakery
Orwashers Bakery
Super Nice Coffee and
 Bakery

Ice Cream/Sweets
Big Gay Ice Cream
Delillo Pastry Shop
Emack & Bolio's
Sedutto
Sugar Hill Creamery

19. Native Noodles

2129 Amsterdam Avenue, Washington Heights

One of the city's few strictly Singaporean cafés is tucked away in a relatively quiet corner of Washington Heights, with a comfortable interior and dishes handed through a window from the kitchen. There are noodles galore, including laksa and peanut satay noodles, but look to fritters, dumplings, and buns for smaller feeds. The roti john sandwich is a unique delight, a hero of ground-beef omelet with spicy ketchup and caramelized onions.

20. Red Rooster

310 Lenox Avenue, Harlem

World-renowned chef Marcus Samuelsson opened this splashy upscale restaurant more than a decade ago in Harlem, and it has stayed busy ever since. Pulling from his Ethiopian and Swedish roots and the culture of the neighborhood, the restaurant's menu rotates between shrimp and grits with a tomato-okra stew, pan-fried catfish with black-eyed peas, and a twenty-piece chicken tower with corn bread and sides. This is a great option if you're looking for a spot to dress up a bit for.

21. Schaller & Weber

1654 2nd Avenue #1, Upper East Side

This butcher shop first opened back when Yorkville, the most eastern part of the Upper East Side, was still teeming with businesses run by German immigrants. The neighborhood has changed dramatically, but this German market selling sausages and other charcuterie is still going strong. Next door, the team has a sausage bar selling bratwurst with toppings like curry ketchup, sauerkraut, and slaw, as well as a swanky cocktail bar called Jeremy's.

22. Sushi Noz

181 East 78th Street, Upper East Side

The Upper East Side's Sushi Noz is considered one of the absolute best omakase spots—and it's also one of the most expensive. Nozomu Abe serves eight guests at a time at his sushi counter at roughly $500 per diner. But it's an unforgettable meal with a masterful level of technique. Come dressed to impress.

23. Sylvia's

328 Malcolm X Boulevard, Harlem

Sylvia's is synonymous with Harlem. More than a soul food restaurant, Sylvia's is a true institution, even long after its namesake owner's passing. What began as a low-key spot in 1962 has since become one of the city's most vital establishments—its ribs, fried chicken, and corn bread are beloved citywide and beyond.

24. Taqueria 86

210 West 94th Street, Upper West Side

The name references the year the World Cup was held in New York City, which makes sense because some championship-level tacos can be found here. It's made to look like a red-and-green vinyl diner, where sports memorabilia covers the walls and televisions blare games. There are ten different tacos available, each nodding to a different region in Mexico: from Ensenada to Sonora. Margaritas, beers, and tequila shots round out the taqueria feel.

25. Tatiana by Kwame Onwuachi
10 Lincoln Center Plaza, Lincoln Square

After closing his restaurants in DC, *Top Chef* star Kwame Onwuachi has returned to his hometown for a swanky new restaurant inside Lincoln Center. The menu pulls from Onwuachi's Bronx roots as well as flavors from the African diaspora: Expect creative spins like curried goat patties, egusi dumplings, pastrami suya, and the Cosmic Brownie, a play on the bodega dessert.

26. Teranga
1280 5th Avenue, East Harlem

Located inside the cultural venue the Africa Center, just off Central Park, Teranga is an ideal spot for an affordable counter-service meal in a colorful, aesthetically pleasing environment that despite its fast-casual format feels nothing like a Chipotle. It's run by big-time Senegalese chef Pierre Thiam and serves up a taste of West Africa through affordable bowls of jollof, efo riro (a red palm oil stew made with okra and kale), spicy plantains, and more.

27. Tom's Restaurant
2880 Broadway, Morningside Heights

You know this diner—and its red glowing signage—as the resident clubhouse on *Seinfeld*. But these days, Tom's Restaurant—open since the 1940s—services the university crowd. This no-frills establishment has all the Americana diner classics: omelets served any time of day, milkshakes, and a lumberjack plate with sausage links, pancakes, and bacon.

QR CODES for our online guides to **UPTOWN** neighborhoods:

HARLEM

UPPER EAST SIDE

UPPER WEST SIDE

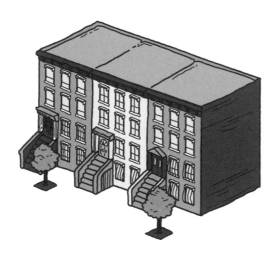

UPTOWN
SHOPPING

In the area of Manhattan surrounding Central Park, you'll find many of the city's most famous cultural institutions. Farther north, the National Jazz Museum in Harlem and the Cloisters beyond have been attracting visitors from New York and much farther afield for decades. The shops that merit a visit exist in much the same spirit as these long-standing beacons of the city. From the Jewish appetizing store that cameoed in *You've Got Mail* to the century-old family businesses of the Bronx's Little Italy (considered by many to be New York's "real" Italian center, with its dozens of decades-old shops and restaurants), many of these are places that have stood the test of time precisely because they are worth a special trip, while others feel a part of the fabric of their neighborhoods, even if they haven't yet accrued quite as many years.

1. Harlem Chocolate Factory
2363 Adam Clayton Powell Jr. Boulevard, Harlem

Harlem Chocolate Factory has only been open since 2018, but it prides itself on drawing connections to the neighborhood's history. Bonbons are named for neighborhood landmarks, while pretty, giftable chocolate bars are molded into the shape of Strivers' Row town houses.

2. Kee's Chocolates
228 Columbus Avenue, Upper West Side

It would be easy to stroll by this petite Upper West Side shop without realizing that you're passing up some of the best chocolate truffles in the country. In 2002, Kee Ling Tong left a corporate job to make handcrafted chocolates, eventually growing to a few locations in Manhattan. Now this tiny storefront is the only one open. And while chocolate bars and barks in flavors like ginger salt and sesame ship nationwide, Kee's doesn't ship its bonbons or truffles, so an in-person visit is a must.

3. Kitchen Arts & Letters
1435 Lexington Avenue, Upper East Side

A store for cookbooks, food scholarship, and food writing more broadly, Kitchen Arts & Letters has counted James Beard and Julia Child among its customers, not to mention countless influential chefs who have come since. Those customers come to the Upper East Side shop for new books, old books, rare books, and the guidance of the Kitchen Arts & Letters staff, who always have an opinion to share. It's also a library of sorts, as not all the books on hand are actually for sale. Owner Nach Waxman told Eater in 2014, on the heels of the store's thirtieth anniversary, "There are books that we simply don't admit to having because we're waiting for the right customer."

4. Mondel Chocolates
2913 Broadway, Morningside Heights

In 2016, Robert Sietsema counted Mondel Chocolates among the last of the city's old-fashioned chocolate shops of the ilk that proliferated in the 1940s. Back then, according to Mondel lore, this shop was a favorite of actress Katharine Hepburn's. These days, it's patronized by the Columbia University community for gifts of chocolate truffles, fudge, nutty chocolate barks, and turtles.

5. William Greenberg Desserts
1100 Madison Avenue, Upper East Side

Kosher bakery William Greenberg is known for having the best black-and-white cookies in the city, the iced, cake-like confection that's one of the foods most symbolic of New York. But there are other desserts here, many available in gift tins perfect for taking home, wherever that may be. The sticky-bun-like schnecken are a customer favorite, and the brownies are renowned enough to have made an appearance on a 2012 episode of *Mad Men*.

6. Zabar's
2245 Broadway, Upper West Side

The word "iconic" gets thrown around a lot, but it truly applies to Jewish deli and grocery Zabar's, which has occupied the same Upper West Side location for ninety years. For just as long, the Zabar family has supplied New Yorkers with artisanal cheeses, babka, pastrami, caviar, and expertly sliced smoked fish, among other delicacies. Their name has reached such renown you'll find it on packaged goods and merchandise practically tailor-made to take home as a New York souvenir.

BODEGAS 101

By Luke Fortney

Traces of the New York City that appears in movies and on television—the freewheeling "city that never sleeps"—still exist, but they can be harder to find as gentrification, real estate development, a pandemic, and other forces change the face of this dynamic city. One sure-fire way to see something weird? Step into your local bodega.

There's no one-to-one equivalent for these all-purpose general stores elsewhere in the United States, the closest thing being maybe a 7-Eleven. Much like the international chain of convenience stores, bodegas sell just about everything you would need for both a trip to the airport and a long subway ride home after a bad first date. Aisles are crowded with Flamin' Hot snacks, over-the-counter medicines, travel-sized toiletries, and—wait, is that a stray cat? In lieu of a conveyor belt of twirling taquitos, you're likely to find a late-night grill and a line cook who knows his sandwiches as well as some career bartenders know their drinks.

It's been said that the subway system is one of New York City's great equalizers, a vast network of tunnels and railways where Wall Street executives, unhoused New Yorkers, college students, police officers, Chinatown aunties, and Williamsburg hipsters are briefly forced to occupy the same space. It's true, and by a similar token, the same can be said about the city's collection of bodegas. Between the wooden aisles of these neighborhood stores, New Yorkers begin their days, end their nights, grocery shop, and cure hangovers with some of the city's most iconic, and reasonably priced, foods.

In a city of more than eight million people, the importance of these neighborhood shops can't be overstated. For new New Yorkers, and those who have recently moved within the city, a bodega is often one of the first places they become a "regular." For out-of-towners, the ubiquitous shops can be used to find directions or recommendations within a neighborhood. "Bodegas are like an extension of your house," says Francisco Marte, the founder of the Bodega and Small Business Group, which represents some two thousand of the shops across the city. At Green Earth, a bodega he operates in the Bronx, he runs tabs for families in the neighborhood, knows many of his customers by name, and has memorized even more of their orders. "When I see a customer walking up, I'll start to make their coffee how they like it," he says.

Green Earth closes its doors around midnight, but others stay open around the clock, especially those located along a commercial street or a subway line, like Healthy Bites Gourmet, a bodega in Bed-Stuy where some of the shop's busiest hours are in the minutes after bars in the Brooklyn neighborhood have closed. On a Friday at four A.M., expect to see a line that stretches toward the door. A menu with sandwiches, wraps, salads, juices, and countless other items spans one wall of the establishment, but it's not uncommon to hear customers ask for off-menu items with exacting specifications.

"Can I get two chopped cheeses on a roll with meat, cheese, ketchup, mayo, and jalapeños?" a customer said on a recent evening. "No lettuce or tomato."

Unlike the way many of us talk about restaurants, there's no best bodega in the city—but there's certainly a best bodega for the occasion. The knowledge of who makes the best chopped cheese, yaroas (fries smothered in toppings), chimis (a Dominican hamburger), and chicken over rice in a neighborhood—these are badges of honor earned through meals good and bad over the years. "For those of us from the 'hood, knowing what to order and where is a huge source of pride," says New York state senator Jessica Ramos, who recalls concluding nights out at salsa clubs in her twenties with meals at Dominican bodegas in Queens.

Indeed, bodegas have spawned entire subcultures of food within the city. The bacon, egg, and cheese—a sandwich that's often written, but rarely said aloud, as a BEC—is one. Another is the chopped cheese, a sandwich made from minced beef, melted cheese, lettuce, tomato, ketchup, and mayonnaise on a hero that originated on the flat-top grills of a Harlem bodega named Blue Sky Deli, formerly Hajji's. Both of these sandwiches, and many others that you'll encounter at a bodega, can be ordered for a few dollars each.

"This is an essential New York experience, but let's not get crazy here," says Eric Huang, a former sous chef at Eleven Madison Park who made a habit of eating bacon, egg, and cheese sandwiches with mayonnaise and avocado from a bodega before his shifts at the three-Michelin-starred restaurant. "It's mediocre bacon, a couple eggs cooked on a flat-top, on a Kaiser roll, with American cheese, but it's part of the rhythm of life here."

How many bodegas are there? No one can agree

Bodegas can be found in all five boroughs, sometimes two or more to an intersection, but an exact count has eluded New Yorkers for years. In 2018, the most recent year that city officials have data on record, the Department of Health and Mental Hygiene estimated there were roughly seven thousand bodegas in the five boroughs, though experts say the number is likely much higher. In 2021, a writer for a local food publication, Grub Street, used public and online records to argue that the total was closer to eight thousand. Later that same year, Bloomberg put the count at around thirteen thousand.

Part of the difficulty is that no one can agree on what, exactly, makes a bodega a bodega. That name, which comes from the Spanish word for "warehouse" or "wine cellar," is used by fewer than twenty businesses in New York City. Half of the city's "bodegas" refer to themselves as "delis," "grills," or "groceries" in their names, often accompanied by a word like "organic," "gourmet," or "natural." The Department of Health has an official definition for the shops—any store under four thousand square feet that sells milk, meat, or eggs and is not a part of a major chain qualifies—but a spokesperson for the agency admits it's just one of a handful of ways one can classify them.

Left to their own devices, New Yorkers have filled in the blank with definitions rooted in pride and personal experience to distinguish these shops from neighborhood convenience stores, smoke shops, and other businesses that sell similar items. "You know a bodega when you see one," says Huang, who grew up in Manhattan, Queens, and Long Island and now runs a fried chicken restaurant called Pecking House in Brooklyn. He's developed criteria for picking out bodegas: They have to have a deli counter, for one, but he also expects to find certain household odds and ends, like cigarettes, individual rolls of toilet paper, bags of cat litter, and a small selection of fresh produce.

A checklist of qualifying and eliminating factors like Huang's—is there a bodega cat hanging around the register? Is the storefront too new?—lies in the hearts of most New Yorkers, some more forgiving than others. "As long as it has a little bit of everything, I consider it a bodega," says Marte of the Bodega and Small Business Group.

Bodega food is more than bacon, egg, and cheese

Over the past century, bodegas have evolved to meet the needs of their neighborhoods, arriving at the corner delis and grills New Yorkers know today. The city's earliest bodegas date back to the beginning of the twentieth century, when Spanish-speaking immigrants arrived in New York and used the word to refer to small shops that sold a variety of items, including cigarettes, newspapers, and candy. By the end of World War II, as the city's Latin immigrant population continued to grow, bodegas selling prepared foods, imported ingredients, and beer had started to become more common.

Fast-forward and today New York bodegas are run by owners from Puerto Rican, Yemeni, Dominican, Mexican, and other immigrant groups. All have brought their own twist to the New York staple:

In bodegas with Muslim owners, alcohol is not usually found, but a larger selection of nonalcoholic drinks might be, while some Korean grocers sell fruit and flowers in front of their premises. "No two bodegas are created equal," says Senator Ramos. "They are an expression of a neighborhood."

In Brooklyn, bodega manager Neil Córdova and his family have been running Reyes Deli & Grocery, a Mexican bodega in the borough's Park Slope neighborhood, since 2007. In addition to the usual deli sandwiches found at bodegas across the city, the menu includes tacos and burritos made with Mexican meats, including chorizo, carnitas, cecina, and longaniza purchased from local butchers or prepared in-house. On weekends, barbacoa is sold by the pound from a counter that also sells lottery tickets, and hundreds of homemade tamales are offered with fillings like pork and chicken mole for a few dollars each. Everything sells out.

"It started with tacos and tortas," Córdova says. As his neighbors in Park Slope caught wind of the shop's larger ambitions, the menu continued to grow.

On Second Avenue, in Manhattan's East Village neighborhood, Pak Punjab Deli & Grocery caters to taxi drivers and the neighborhood's rowdy late-night crowd with its twenty-four-hour menu of prepared Pakistani foods, most of which are available for under $10. Aluminum containers packed with chicken biryani, vegetable samosas, lamb curries, and flaky fried fish speckled with sesame seeds are dispensed around the clock. Even here, it's possible to order an egg and cheese sandwich, sans bacon, on a roll for breakfast, lunch, or dinner.

Bodega Pride

It might seem like a lot of fuss, but New Yorkers take a great deal of pride in these all-day corner stores. When Punjabi Deli (page 37), a Lower East Side storefront that toes the line between counter-service restaurant and bodega—a rail runs along one wall for eating indoors while standing, and a smaller selection of snacks and sodas are sold behind the counter—was at risk of closing during the pandemic, fans of the shop banded together to raise more than $50,000 to keep its doors open.

"It's a real thing," says Huang of Pecking House, reflecting on one of his favorite bodegas in the neighborhood, the late-night Healthy Bites Gourmet in Bed-Stuy. "You feel some ownership and belonging for this place."

Bodega owners look out for customers when they're at their most vulnerable—that is, ordering a BEC with mayonnaise before heading into a shift at one of the world's best restaurants—and in turn, their customers look out for them. From behind a sneeze guard in Park Slope, Córdova has been there to see his patrons at Reyes Deli & Grocery go through breakups, grow their families, and get married. "Some of them, one of the first things they do afterward is come by the shop for tacos," he says.

What These New Yorkers Order at Bodegas

Eric Huang
Former sous chef at Eleven Madison Park and owner of Pecking House

A bacon, egg, and cheese with mayo and avocado.

Jessica Ramos
New York State senator, District 13

Yaroa, a Dominican street food made from French fries or plantains that are topped with meat, cheese, and condiments like mayo and ketchup.

Neil Córdova
Manager at Reyes Deli & Grocery in Brooklyn

A bacon, egg, and cheese with hot sauce and avocado.

Francisco Marte
Owner of Green Earth in the Bronx

A turkey sandwich with Muenster cheese, lettuce, and tomato

Bodega Vocabulary

BEC: A sandwich with bacon, egg, and cheese that can be ordered at any time of day. They are most commonly ordered on a bagel or a Kaiser roll.

Bodega cat: A domestic cat or a street cat that an owner has endeared itself to with food in a bid to ward off rats and other pests. Bodega cats have been outlawed by city health officials, but it's not uncommon to see them roaming the aisles of a neighborhood deli.

Chicken over rice: A platter of chicken or lamb gyro, yellow rice, and a side salad. Squiggles of red and white sauce can be added on top.

Chopped cheese: A sandwich that originated in Harlem made from ground beef, onions, melted cheese, lettuce, tomatoes, ketchup, and mayonnaise. Also called a chop cheese.

Hero: A longer bread roll that's similar to a hoagie or a submarine sandwich. The term can be used to refer to hot and cold sandwiches.

Roll: A Kaiser roll, also called a Vienna roll. Smaller than a hero, and one of the most common bread options for a sandwich at a bodega.

SPK: An acronym for salt, pepper, and ketchup. A common addition to bodega sandwiches.

SPOTLIGHT: THE BRONX

The Bronx has always been a culinary destination, from some of the city's best street food to the Italian district of Arthur Avenue, with plenty of great spots clustered near the New York Botanical Garden and the Bronx Zoo. Farther south, easily accessible by trains, are areas like Mott Haven, a sprawling neighborhood with a diverse population—and, accordingly, a medley of cuisines.

DINING

188 Bakery Cuchifritos
158 East 188th Street, Fordham Heights
When Jose Coto took over this Puerto Rican and Dominican lunch counter back in the 1980s, restaurants devoted to cuchifritos—a word that usually refers to fried meat, typically pork—were more common in New York City. Coto keeps the tradition alive masterfully. Saddle up to the fluorescent-lit barstool seats and pick from a dozen options listed on blue-and-red handmade signs that line the wall like wallpaper.

Fauzia's Heavenly Delights
East 161st Street & Concourse Village West, Melrose
This Jamaican food truck has been in business for nearly thirty years, more recently taken over by the owner's daughter, Fauzia Aminah Rasheed. The menu is entirely halal and includes dishes like jerk chicken gyros that blend Jamaican cuisine with New York food-truck staples.

Liebman's Deli
552 West 235th Street, Kingsbridge
This Bronx favorite is a slice of Jewish history, opened by Joe Liebman in 1953 and now run by the Dekel family. Hefty sandwiches are loaded with pastrami and corned beef, both cured on-site.

Louie & Ernie's Pizza
1300 Crosby Avenue, Pelham Bay
Open for more than sixty years, Louie & Ernie's won't quit serving up some of the best slices of thin-crust pizza in NYC. The crowd favorites here are the white and sausage-topped pies.

Papaye
Multiple locations
Papaye ("doing good") is a long-running Ghanaian diner with the dishes posted prominently over the steam-table counter. Jollof rice with stewed chicken or fried fish is a good bet.

Roberto's
603 Crescent Avenue, Belmont
When Roberto Paciullo established his eponymous restaurant in 1989, it was surprising: There among the red-sauce joints of Arthur Avenue was a different kind of Italian restaurant, closely approximating a roadside rural trattoria. Check the chalkboard

specials, which might include radiatori in cartoccio or fricasseed rabbit.

Zero Otto Nove
2357 Arthur Avenue, Belmont

Zero Otto Nove is owned by a Salerno native, and serves perfectly crisp wood-fired pies with ingredients like soppressata, capers, anchovies, and bubbling fontina cheese. In addition to pies, Zero Otto Nove is also home to an incredible chicken capriccioso, with mozzarella from the acclaimed Casa Della Mozzarella down the street. This location in the Bronx's Little Italy is worth the trip, but note there's a second location in Flatiron.

SHOPPING

Arthur Avenue Retail Market
2344 Arthur Avenue, Belmont

In the heart of the Bronx's Little Italy, bakeries, butcher shops, pasta shops, restaurants, delis, and other vendors of Italian specialties sit inside a "wonderfully graceless concrete structure," as Robert Sietsema once put it. Many of the vendors have been here for as long as the market itself, which was opened in 1940 as part of a citywide effort to move pushcart vendors inside. And these days you can follow up an order of eggplant parmigiana at TV-famous Mike's Deli (one of those original vendors) with a beer at the newer Bronx Beer Hall or even a freshly rolled cigar at La Casa Grande or Valentin Cigars.

Borgatti's Ravioli and Egg Noodles
632 East 187th Street, Belmont

Fresh pasta shop Borgatti's has been just off Arthur Avenue since 1935, several years after Lindo and Maria Borgatti immigrated to America from Bologna. The business remains in the Borgatti family, selling fresh ravioli, manicotti, and cavatelli, but also gift boxes of fettuccine in varieties like lemon pepper, basil, and tomato.

Calabria Pork Store
2338 Arthur Avenue, Belmont

On the Bronx's Arthur Avenue, Calabria Pork Store is worth a visit almost as much for the spectacle of hundreds of sausages hanging from the ceiling as for the sausage itself. But if you're making the trip, you'll want to leave with some of the shop's dry sausage, soppressata, pancetta, or prosciutto.

Teitel Brothers
2372 Arthur Avenue, Belmont

As tends to be tradition on Arthur Avenue, Teitel Brothers has been operated by the same family since it opened in 1915. The original Teitel brothers, Jewish-Austrian immigrants Jacob and Morris (note the tiled Star of David at the shop's entrance), opened the shop to sell a variety of imported Italian specialties, like olive oil, canned tomatoes, and cheese. The current generation of Teitel brothers still imports from Italy and has branched out a bit, with items sourced domestically and even farther afield, like Croatian wafer cookies.

QR CODE for our online guide to the Bronx:

ARTHUR AVENUE

Astoria
Corona
Elmhurst
Flushing
Forest Hills
Jackson Heights
Jamaica
Long Island City
Richmond Hill
Ridgewood
Rockaway Beach
Sunnyside
Woodside

QUE

ENS 5

QUEENS

DINING

1. 969 NYC Coffee
2. Arepa Lady
3. Astoria Seafood
4. Ayada
5. Birria-Landia
6. Bolivian Llama Party
7. Caleta 111 Cevicheria
8. Casa Enrique
9. Corona Plaza
10. Eddie's Sweet Shop
11. Evelia's Tamales
12. Haidilao
13. Jackson Diner
14. The Lemon Ice King of Corona
15. Mariscos El Submarino
16. Nan Xiang Xiao Long Bao
17. Nepali Bhanchha Ghar
18. New World Mall
19. Pupusas Ridgewood
20. Rolo's
21. Ruta Oaxaca
22. Sami's Kabab House
23. Sushi on Me
24. Tacoway Beach
25. Taiwanese Gourmet
26. Taverna Kyclades
27. Temple Canteen
28. Tong
29. While in Kathmandu
30. White Bear
31. Zaab Zaab

SHOPPING

1. Aigner Chocolates
2. Earth & Me
3. Lockwood
4. Mogmog
5. New World Mall
6. Parrot Coffee
7. Phil-Am Food Mart
8. Rio Market
9. Slovak-Czech Varieties

QUEENS
DINING

There's nowhere else in the universe, let alone the city, that allows you to get a taste for so many cultures and languages all at once as Queens. There's really no way to try to eat through this borough in one day, but even scoping out one neighborhood—or a street especially dense with restaurants—will give you plenty to try. Astoria is often known for its Greek food, which it has en masse, but main thoroughfares like Steinway Street and Ditmars Boulevard are also home to Egyptian, Lebanese, Moroccan, and other cuisines. Flushing is where you'll find some of the most spectacular hot pot, Sichuan food, and dim sum parlors, as well as plenty of Korean barbecue. Ridgewood, a rapidly gentrifying neighborhood that was once primarily Polish and Latin American, also boasts some of the borough's most talked-about (and pricier) new restaurants and bars. Elmhurst has excellent Thai and Malaysian food, as well as dessert spots to match. Jackson Heights is likely the best Queens neighborhood for street food: It's home to Little India, but also offers other South Asian food like Nepalese as well as South American, Southeast Asian, and Latin American.

Overall, Queens is way more low-key than its other borough counterparts, and unlike Brooklyn and Manhattan in particular, this is a great area to dine around where you don't need to stress about making a reservation in advance: Most lean on the more casual end of the spectrum. Just be ready with cash on hand. Seemingly everywhere you turn your head there's something delicious to eat in Queens, be it street-side, in a restaurant, or tucked below street level in the subway, no matter the time of day.

1. 969 NYC Coffee

37-61 80th Street,
Jackson Heights

Since opening in Jackson Heights in 2016, 969 NYC Coffee has been a favorite of neighborhood regulars—both for its onigirazu (a rice-based sandwich) and for its genial owner, Mitsumine Oda. Though it serves coffee, it's really known for its Japanese snacks. There's no menu, but try an onigirazu with chicken katsu or shrimp patty variations, layered with avocado, carrots, and American cheese, and one of the heart-shaped onigiri 969 has come to be known for.

2. Arepa Lady

77-17 37th Avenue,
Jackson Heights

Maria Piedad Cano—who fled from violence in Colombia decades ago to make a better life—used to sell her beloved arepas at a cart underneath the 7 train. Inspired by the intense popularity of her food, she expanded to bigger digs, eventually relocating the restaurant to its current iteration, which is a family affair. There are several arepas (shown opposite) to choose from, including relleno, queso, and chorizo.

3. Astoria Seafood

37-10 33rd Street,
Astoria

If you're looking for an interactive experience, Astoria Seafood is like no other in the city. Essentially it's a fish market; point to your seafood of choice and have it prepared for you right on the spot—all you have to do is tell them how you want it cooked. Dining here is pretty reasonably priced, and it can be especially fun when bringing your own drinks, since it's BYOB.

4. Ayada

7708 Woodside Avenue,
Elmhurst

At many Thai restaurants in New York, flavors are dialed down for Western preferences—but at Ayada, the heat is turned to full volume. Located in a part of Elmhurst brimming with Thai food, it's the best place in the city to have a truly tantalizing Thai food experience. Now more than fifteen years old, Ayada is still serving an ambitious menu of larb salads, whole fish, and sour curry in a dining room covered in photos of Thai dignitaries.

5. Birria-Landia

77-99 Roosevelt Avenue,
Jackson Heights

Birria-Landia opened as a food truck below the subway platform in Jackson Heights with a focus on saucy, cheesy tacos de birria, marked by red tortillas, with cups of consommé. Birria is said to have started in the Mexican state of Jalisco, but its evolution onto tacos is credited to Tijuana. At Birria-Landia, José Moreno, a Del Posto alum and Puebla native, puts his own spin on the dish to critical acclaim. Its popularity has led to a rise in birria operations across the city.

6. Bolivian Llama Party

44-14 48th Avenue,
Sunnyside

Originally operating as sandwich counters in Manhattan and Brooklyn, this fast-casual restaurant is better than ever in Queens. Now in Sunnyside, an area marked by its Colombian and Ecuadorian restaurants, Bolivian Llama Party serves perfect salteñas, pastries stuffed with meat or vegan with jackfruit, with crust made yellow from aji amarillo, twisted closed like a savory clutch purse. There are also bowls with Bolivian pork shoulder, papitas (fries with spicy mayo), and fried chicharron strips.

7. Caleta 111 Cevicheria

111-27 Jamaica Avenue,
Richmond Hill

Peruvian ceviche is the name of the game at Caleta 111 in Queens's Richmond Hill. Chef Luis Caballero offers his own slice of Lima, where the garlicky, tangy tiger's milk is the backbone of its ceviches and gives them their signature pucker-up tart marinade. Ceviches—elegantly plated here as any fine-dining establishment—can be customized to one's liking with a smattering of seafood options.

8. Casa Enrique
5-48 49th Avenue,
Long Island City
Michelin-rated Casa Enrique opened in Long Island City in 2012 and quickly became a local hot spot. Chef Cosme Aguilar is the draw, as he assembles tacos with the care of a sushi chef, wrapping ethereal tortillas around minimally adorned proteins. The casual dining room is often packed with locals, fútbol fans, and other patrons for whom Casa Enrique is destination dining. Go for the mole de Piaxtla (a mole poblano named after the town where the chef's father grew up) or the pork hominy pozole, as well as the top-tier tacos.

9. Corona Plaza
40-04 National Street,
Corona
Located underneath the 103rd Street–Corona Plaza station, a vibrant array of Latin American food stands here serve everything from churros to tacos and aguas frescas. It's one of the only markets in the city actually run by a vendor association (not a third party), and the workers here are fighting against the red tape and harassment their businesses often face. It's also a space to try some of the city's best street food.

10. Eddie's Sweet Shop
105-29 Metropolitan Avenue #1,
Forest Hills
Eddie's Sweet Shop in Forest Hills is more than a spot that serves ice cream—that's homemade, no less—it's also a neighborhood hangout. This is definitely a spot to get a sundae with whipped cream and the requisite maraschino cherry. An ice cream parlor has existed at the property since the 1940s, but in 1968, it became Eddie's, now operated by the owner Giuseppe Citrano's son.

11. Evelia's Tamales
96-09 Northern Boulevard,
Elmhurst
Evelia Coyotzi has had a tamales cart in Corona, Queens, for decades, but it was only in 2022 that she opened a brick-and-mortar in East Elmhurst. There she serves tamales with fillings like mole, queso, and sweet pineapple alongside an expanded all-day Mexican breakfast menu of eggs with ham, rice and beans, tortas, quesadillas, and the masa-based drink atole.

12. Haidilao
138-23 39th Avenue,
Flushing
There are dozens of hot pot restaurants to choose from in NYC, but few if any can also say they offer a toy doll to sit with patrons who arrive alone, apparently to seem less lonely (hot pot is usually a group activity, after all). That's not the only entertaining element at this Flushing favorite that Eater critic Robert Sietsema calls an "adult playground": Theatrics extend to live performance noodle pulls, and there are also board games, free snacks for waiting customers, and even a massage station. It's the first New York outpost of a Chinese chain, now located in more than a dozen countries.

13. Jackson Diner
37-47 74th Street,
Jackson Heights
Jackson Heights is home to Little India, and one of its more popular establishments is this Indian diner. Open since 1980, Jackson Diner is an all-ages-friendly option that offers Indian cooking in a super-casual environment. Over the years, it has attracted major politicians and celebrities, who have dined on delicacies like garlic chile shrimp, gobi Manchurian, and chicken korma. Afterward, stop into the South Asian supermarket Patel Brothers to pick up snacks for the train ride.

14. The Lemon Ice King of Corona
52-02 108th Street,
Corona

For more than sixty years, the Lemon Ice King of Corona has been cooling down summer heat with its Italian ices (shown above). Creamy, smooth, and served in paper cups, the unique texture is achieved without any dairy. This cash-only favorite has more traditional Italian flavors like pistachio and lemon, but these days also includes sour apple, piña colada, peanut butter, and bubble gum.

15. Mariscos El Submarino
88-05 Roosevelt Avenue,
Jackson Heights

Mexican seafood, known as mariscos, was once harder to come by in New York City. Mariscos El Submarino in Jackson Heights is a fun primer and not just because of its logo with a mustachioed submarine. Make sure to order one of the towering seafood tostadas, or a parfait glass filled with Clamato and shrimp that comes with buttery saltines for dipping. Or go for spicy aguachile negro that comes with shrimp and other seafood in a hefty molcajete—a favorite hangover food in Mexico.

16. Nan Xiang Xiao Long Bao
39-16 Prince Street,
Flushing

Nan Xiang Xiao Long Bao— a name that nods to the Nanxiang region of Shanghai—made soup dumplings a cult favorite among New Yorkers when it opened its doors in Flushing back in 2006. These days, soup dumplings can be found across the city much more readily, but this spot is worth a dedicated visit.

17. Nepali Bhanchha Ghar
74-15 Roosevelt Avenue,
Jackson Heights

Nepali Bhanchha Ghar has been serving thali plates and noodle soups since 2015, under the helm of owner Yamuna Shrestha, who immigrated to Jackson Heights from Syangja, Nepal. One specialty is their much celebrated momos, served steamed, fried, or in a spicy, warming jhola broth. There's also sel roti, rings of rice flour sweet bread, deep-fried in ghee and served with spicy, funky chutney; a selection of BBQ skewers; or sukuti, Himalayan jerky.

18. New World Mall
136-20 Roosevelt Avenue,
Flushing

In the basement of this multifloor shopping mall at the center of downtown Flushing, conveniently right off the Main Street 7 train stop, you'll find one of the best food courts in the five boroughs devoted to regional Chinese food. Go to Lanzhou Handmade Noodle for hand-cut and hand-pulled noodles, Laoma Malatang for tofu dry pot, and Mojoilla Fresh for the savory pancakes known as jianbing, with fillings like ham and cheese.

19. Pupusas Ridgewood
71-20 Fresh Pond Road,
Ridgewood

One of the best fast-casual experiences in Ridgewood is Pupusas Ridgewood, which serves at least a dozen types of Salvadoran pupusas—bigger than most in the city—that come with a crunchy slaw and vinegary hot sauce. There are no tables inside, but on a warm day, sit on one of the street-side tables and nosh on pupusas with pork rinds or chicken mole, or one of the many vegetarian options, like zucchini, queso, or spinach.

20. Rolo's

853 Onderdonk Avenue,
Ridgewood

Opened by Gramercy Tavern vets, Rolo's doesn't keep to one cuisine, though the backbone is Italian wood-fire cooking. The knockout double cheeseburger has grilled onions and a Dijon mayo with a pickled hot pepper, there's a green lasagna served more like a wide pancake rather than a tower, polenta bread comes wood-fired with Calabrian chile butter, and crispy potatoes "war style" are essentially potato wedges with an Indonesian peanut sauce.

21. Ruta Oaxaca

35-03 Broadway,
Astoria

The Mexican state of Oaxaca is known for its complex moles, which are the star at this Astoria restaurant. Inside a mural-clad dining room with plenty of outdoor seating, find moles like the deep brown mole Oaxaca (often listed as a mole negro) doused on dishes like a chicken enchilada, as well as lesser-seen versions like a mole amarillo or mole verde.

22. Sami's Kabab House

35-57 Crescent Street,
Astoria

Enter through a takeout area on Crescent Street and find a full-service restaurant, which feels like a family's home dining room, connected through the side. Yes, there are of course kebabs on the Afghan menu, but the aushak dumplings and the kabuli pulao, a stewed lamb dish over rice studded with strips of carrots and raisins, both deserve attention. There's a follow-up location in Long Island City.

23. Sushi on Me

71-26 Roosevelt Avenue,
Jackson Heights

In a city where sushi bros rule omakase, Sushi on Me is a place for the rest of us. A raucous dinner party located in a secret-ish Jackson Heights basement, this cash-only sushi spot is not only one of the best deals for omakase, but it's really unlike the quiet, monastic sushi spots that fill the city. Music, shouting, and lots of spilled sake are to be expected. They now also have a second location in Williamsburg.

24. Tacoway Beach

302 Beach 87th Street,
Rockaway Beach

Some of the best fish tacos in NYC are at this summertime taco shack, just a few blocks from the boardwalk in the Rockaways. No beach trip to this strip of Queens is complete without a visit to Tacoway, which in addition to fish tacos has plenty of veggie options, as well as sides like elote, roasted corn slathered in mayo, lime, and cotija cheese. For drinks, there are options like fresh pineapple-mint juice, as well as some of the area's best margaritas.

25. Taiwanese Gourmet

8402 Broadway,
Elmhurst

These days, new Taiwanese restaurants span every borough of the city. But more than forty years ago, Elmhurst's Taiwanese Gourmet mainly stood alone. Located in one of NYC's several Chinatowns, this checkerboard-floored dining room with communal tables serves family-style portions of fly's head, pork rolls, and three-cup chicken. It's BYOB, so bring whatever bottle tickles your fancy.

26. Taverna Kyclades

36-01 Ditmars Boulevard,
Astoria

If there's one Greek restaurant you need to stop at in Astoria, it has to be Taverna Kyclades. At this kitchen straight out of *Mamma Mia!*, order homey, family-style dishes like spanakopita, tzatziki dip, stuffed grape leaves, swordfish kebabs, and more. They have locations with the same menu and similar vibes in the East Village and in Bayside.

27. Temple Canteen

143-09 Holly Avenue,
Flushing

Located in a Flushing basement below Ganesh Temple,

this restaurant has been serving some of the best vegetarian food in NYC since opening in 1993. It's essentially a cafeteria, with communal tables and food served on paper plates with plastic trays. Expect nourishing South Indian dishes like yogurt rice, chile masala dosa (shown below), crunchy pakora, and vegetable uttapam. Ask for extra chutney.

28. Tong
153-35B Hillside Avenue, Jamaica
A street food cart sensation, Tong is known for its fuchka—a crunchy bowl-like street food staple of Bangladesh. In addition to those food carts that are now all over Queens and the Bronx, Tong also has a restaurant with seats in Jamaica, Queens, where you can get an expanded menu alongside flaming—yes, flaming—fuchka to light up your day.

29. While in Kathmandu
758 Seneca Avenue, Ridgewood
Right off the Seneca M train stop is this restaurant that serves modern spins on Nepalese staples. There's naan stuffed with cheese, jhol momo (with mushrooms, plantains, chicken, or pork), chile pepper poppers, roti with jerky-style chicken, and fried tilapia with masala fries. The kitsch of the environment—the dining room includes a kitchen in a built-out hut—only adds to how good the food is.

30. White Bear
135-02 Roosevelt Avenue, Flushing
If there's one place you're stopping for dumplings in Queens, it's White Bear. Easily accessible from the Flushing Main Street 7 train stop, this order-at-the-counter spot has virtually no seats, but that won't matter when you find yourself scarfing down dumplings—there are ten to an order—and tons of other noodle dishes at lightning speed. Bring cash.

31. Zaab Zaab
76-04 Woodside Avenue, Jackson Heights
With locations in Elmhurst, Flushing, and Williamsburg, Brooklyn, Zaab Zaab's menu focuses on the Isan region of Thailand. The space is colorfully decorated and fun, but it's not for the faint of heart: Even our critic finds it to be one of the city's spiciest spots. Don't sleep on the offaly larb ped udon.

QR CODES for our online guides to **QUEENS** neighborhoods:

ASTORIA

FLUSHING'S CHINATOWN

JACKSON HEIGHTS

LONG ISLAND CITY

QUEENS
SHOPPING

When extolling the virtues of the city, many New Yorkers are apt to point out that if there's a cuisine they want to eat, there is a business somewhere in the five boroughs that supplies it. Arguably, most of those businesses can be found in just one borough: Queens.

Queens is not just the most ethnically diverse borough in New York, but the most diverse urban area in the world. For starters, there's a Chinatown in Flushing, in 2022 a street in Woodside was renamed Little Manila Avenue, and Astoria is home to both a sizable Greek population and a few blocks known as Little Brazil. In many of these enclaves, you'll find a grocery store that specializes in imports from a faraway home country, meaning international snacks are just a subway ride away. But Queens is also home to those who don't move to be a part of any specific community, but rather for the openness to all that Queens promises, and this, too, is reflected in the variety of shopping you'll find.

1. Aigner Chocolates

103-02 Metropolitan Avenue, Forest Hills

This Forest Hills chocolate shop has been around since 1930, making it one of the oldest chocolate shops in New York City. In 2015, it changed hands, leaving the Aigner family. But new owners Mark Libertini and Rachel Kellner have carried on the Austrian-style chocolate-making tradition, using in part the same equipment that's been around since the shop's early years to make Vienna truffles, nonpareils, cordials, and chocolate barks.

2. Earth & Me

30-38 Steinway Street, Astoria

Earth & Me is a store with a mission: Everything here is in service of living a more environmentally friendly lifestyle. Part of the Astoria shop is a refillery, where regular customers can buy packaging-free cleaning and personal care products. But there's also plenty for the visitor to shop, such as cute reusable dishcloths, beeswax candles, and upcycled coasters, and supplies to make our most-used kitchen items last longer. Simply browsing the array of products presents a breadth of possibilities for a greener kitchen.

3. Lockwood

32-15 33rd Street, Astoria

Since 2013, Lockwood has expanded to five brick-and-mortar locations in Queens and North Brooklyn, but this is the one that started it all. Gifts are Lockwood's bread and butter, and truly you'll find something for anyone you need to shop for. For the hosts, kitchen tools and dining decor run the gamut from quirky to cute; edible options emphasize fun, as with sparkle maple syrup and potato chip chocolate bars; and in the mug department, pop-culture references abound.

4. Mogmog

5-35 51st Avenue, Long Island City

This Long Island City Japanese market specializes in high-quality fish, which you can purchase dried, fresh, or in prepared bento boxes. But for the person looking for something that might travel a bit better, there are a host of other Japanese ingredients to take home, including high-end seasonings, fruit imported from Japan, and beautiful wagashi from pastry chef Phoebe Ogawa, who makes the confections at a studio in the neighborhood.

5. New World Mall

136-20 Roosevelt Avenue, Flushing

Flushing's New World Mall is perhaps best known for its food court, where you can dine on dumplings, dry pot, boba, and more from Chinese and other Asian cuisines. But while there, you can also shop at Asian retailers, including J-Mart, which offers more than thirty thousand square feet of groceries from America, China, Indonesia, Japan, Korea, the Philippines, and Vietnam.

6. Parrot Coffee

31-12 Ditmars Boulevard, Astoria

Although "coffee" is in the name, Parrot isn't a coffee shop. There are beans sold from barrels, but the real draw is the specialty foods, with a focus on imports from Balkan and Mediterranean countries—including a substantial section for candy and sweets—plus the occasional home good, like Slovenian coffeepots and burek trays. Parrot is also a mini chain with second and third locations in Ridgewood and Sunnyside.

7. Phil-Am Food Mart

4003 70th Street,
Woodside

Phil-Am has been supplying the Woodside community—and Filipinos from outside the neighborhood—with Filipino foodstuffs since 1976. Inside the corner store (you can't miss the forest-green sign), cooked food sits in cases at the back while freezer cases stock items like frozen lumpia. Both their halo-halo, the shaved-ice dessert layered with fruit and candy and topped with ice cream flavored with the purple yam called ube, and their ube baked goods are highly recommended, and the store also stocks everything you could need to make ube anything yourself.

8. Rio Market

32-15 36th Avenue,
Astoria

In a micro-neighborhood known to some as Little Brazil, Rio Market has been selling Brazilian groceries since 1994. The store takes up nearly half of its block on 36th Avenue, meaning there's plenty to shop. An in-store café sells pão de queijo and other ready-to-eat snacks.

9. Slovak-Czech Varieties

10-59 Jackson Avenue,
Long Island City

The name says it all. On wooden shelves in the Long Island City shop, you'll find a variety of specialty foods from the Czech Republic and Slovakia, including teas, sausages, tinned herring, pickles, and sweets. The shop also imports wooden toys and, during the appropriate season, handmade Christmas ornaments.

BEYOND RESTAURANTS

Coffee Shops
Astoria Coffee
Honey Moon Coffee Shop
Little Flower Cafe
Milk & Pull
Sweetleaf Coffee Roasters

Bars
Bohemian Hall and Beer Garden
Donovan's Pub
Dutch Kills
Milo's Yard
Sundown Bar

Bakeries
51st Bakery & Cafe
Cannelle Patisserie
Gong Gan
Rudy's Bakery & Café

Ice Cream/Sweets
Mango Mango Dessert
Max & Mina's Ice Cream
Raja Sweets & Fast Food
Xing Fu Tang

Food Courts
New York Food Court
Tangram Food Hall

A PERFECT TWENTY-FOUR HOURS (AND THEN SOME) IN NYC

By Jaya Saxena

8:30 A.M.

Start the day in Union Square and stop at **Breads Bakery**, which basically revitalized babka when it opened in 2013, turning the traditional sweet, braided cake from a beloved though maybe-always-a-little-dry staple of the High Holiday spread to the city's *it* baked good. It's an absolute must-order. Grab whatever else sings to you and head to Union Square to enjoy your meal on a bench under the trees. Or if you happen to be there on one of the days the **Union Square Greenmarket** (page 44) is running, check out the vibrant offerings of everything from flowers to fresh cheese to wine available from local farmers. Oh, and if you need a bathroom, the one in Barnes & Noble is a savior.

Breads Bakery
18 East 16th Street, Union Square, Manhattan

10:00 A.M.

Get your dumpling fix in the World's Borough: Two subways will get you out of Manhattan and out to Flushing, Queens, quickly but with enough time to let your stomach settle a bit. There you can check out the Unisphere in the middle of Flushing Meadows Corona Park, a stainless-steel behemoth you at the very least recognize from *Men in Black*. One more stop on the 7 train gets you to the center of Flushing's Chinatown. Hit up **Nan Xiang Xiao Long Bao** (page 107), which has been slinging soup dumplings and other Shanghai and Northern Chinese dim sum classics, like pan-fried pork buns and marinated tofu, since 2006.

Nan Xiang Xiao Long Bao
39-16 Prince Street, Flushing, Queens

11:30 A.M.

You can walk by the Old Quaker Meeting House, the oldest part of which was built in 1694, and spend some time wandering through the **New World Mall** (page 107), which mostly consists of J-Mart, a massive Asian grocery store. See if anything whets your appetite at the food court, which features everything from Uyghur cuisine to hand-pulled noodles to bubble tea. For dessert, you can head to **New Flushing Bakery** for a classic egg or coconut tart.

New World Mall
136-20 Roosevelt Avenue, Flushing, Queens

New Flushing Bakery
135-45 Roosevelt Avenue, Flushing, Queens

12:30 P.M.

Working your way back toward Manhattan, stop off in Jackson Heights, which more than any other neighborhood captures the diversity of Queens—and the entire city. You can find basically everyone and everything there, from Mexican birria to Tibetan momo to a plethora of gay bars. Spend some time wandering the streets and popping in wherever, but Indian and South Asian grocery **Patel Brothers** is always worth a visit. Maybe you don't need a twenty-pound sack of lentils today, but don't miss the numerous snack aisles carrying imported masala chips, Parle-G tea cookies, and dozens of crunchy namkeen varieties. Don't forget to say hi to Wink, the penguin statue on Seventy-Fifth Street, who is usually festively dressed by neighbors.

For lunch, get momos at **Nepali Bhanchha Ghar** (page 107). It'll feel like home, even if this is nothing like what's served in your home.

Or you could pay homage to the **Arepa Lady** (page 105), aka Maria Piedad Cano, who began serving arepa de queso and arepa de choclo from a street cart on Roosevelt Avenue in 1986. In 2014, she and her sons opened a brick-and-mortar shop in the neighborhood (now there are locations in Astoria and DeKalb Market Hall, too). The menu has expanded to include patacóns, a Colombian burger, and arepa fillings like chicharron and chorizo, but you can't go wrong with the originals.

Patel Brothers
37-27 74th Street, Jackson Heights, Queens

Nepali Bhanchha Ghar
74-15 Roosevelt Avenue, Jackson Heights, Queens

Arepa Lady
77-17 37th Avenue, Jackson Heights, Queens

2:30 P.M.

Heading back into Manhattan (don't worry, the MTA says it's only a forty-minute subway ride), get off in the East Village and stop at the historic **Veniero's Pasticceria & Caffe** for Italian American pastries like cannoli, sfogliatelle, pignoli, or maybe a slice of their ricotta cheesecake. Down the block, you'll also find **Russo's**, an Italian market where you can buy homemade pasta, fresh mozzarella, or a perfect Italian combo sandwich.

Take your snacks to go and head over to Tompkins Square Park, where you can eat while admiring the street performers, the skateboarders, the Temperance Fountain (built to encourage people to drink water instead of alcohol), or possibly the resident group of red-tailed hawks that occasionally swoop at a pigeon. Then wander south through Alphabet City, a neighborhood rich in countercultural history, with landmarks like the Nuyorican Poets Cafe and the Museum of Reclaimed Urban Space. If you're thirsty, stop by the iconic **Ray's Candy Store**, a neighborhood staple for all kinds of sweets, for an egg cream (shown at right), just to say you had an egg cream.

Veniero's Pasticceria & Caffe
342 East 11th Street, East Village, Manhattan

Russo's
344 East 11th Street, East Village, Manhattan

Ray's Candy Store
113 Avenue A, Alphabet City, Manhattan

5:00 P.M.

South is **Essex Market** (page 43), which has been serving the Lower East Side produce, meat, cheese, and specialty foods for more than one hundred years. You can check out stalls like **Essex Olive & Spice** and **Peoples Wine** before hitting **Dhamaka** (page 36), which changed the Indian food game in New York by focusing on Indian cuisines that haven't often made their way onto American menus. Hits have included pork salad from the state of Meghalaya, sweet peppers stuffed with peanuts that taste almost like sausage, and what many consider the best paneer in the city, grilled with ajwain and other spices, as pillowy soft as the lightest cheesecake. You'll need a reservation for the dining room, but the bar is first-come-first-served and offers snacks and appetizers as well as impeccably made cocktails. Get there right as it opens to make your own happy hour with one of the best bites in the city.

7:30 P.M.

Cross the East River into Brooklyn for dinner (you could even walk over the Williamsburg Bridge, a beautiful view at night!). Your night could go two ways. If you want a quintessential, heavy-hitting night on the town, make a reservation at **Peter Luger Steak House** (page 132). It's been operating in some capacity since 1887, back when Williamsburg was a largely German neighborhood, and walking in feels like you've been knocked back a generation or two. The waiters are famously curt, most of the vegetables are an afterthought, the rooms are loud, and the drinks are strong. Steak houses are not places to experiment, so a dry-aged steak is a must, ordered at most medium rare. Other specialties are the thick-cut bacon, creamed spinach, and a pretty perfect hot fudge sundae. It's cash or debit card only, but rolling out a stack of twenties will just make you feel even more like a big spender.

For a more new-school dinner, make your reservation at **Misi**, a temple to all things pasta from Missy Robbins, who helped usher in a wave of modern Italian cuisine in the city. The restaurant is sleek but always bustling, and features a list of seasonal vegetable-based antipasti and handmade pastas, which you can sometimes see the chefs making in a glass-enclosed pasta room right next to the dining room. Don't skip gelato at the end.

Peter Luger
178 Broadway, Williamsburg, Brooklyn

Misi
329 Kent Avenue, Williamsburg, Brooklyn

10:00 P.M.

Waddle your way out of dinner and head straight to **The Commodore** (page 130) for one, or many, of their retro tropical drinks. The Boat Drink in particular is a classic, a simple dark rum and soda with lime that is always cheap and satisfying. If you feel like barhopping, **Rocka Rolla** is just a few blocks away, serving its famous Coffee Thing, a bourbon-and-coffee slushie that should have taken the place of the espresso martini trend.

The Commodore
366 Metropolitan Avenue, Williamsburg, Brooklyn

Rocka Rolla
486 Metropolitan Avenue, Williamsburg, Brooklyn

12:00 A.M.

By now you might be ready for some dancing. There are plenty of options in the neighborhood, but **Ciao Ciao Disco** has both a *Saturday Night Fever*–esque light-up dance floor on which to live out your John Travolta dreams, and Roman-inspired bruschetta to line your stomach. Order one of their aperitivo-style drinks and pretend you're in Trastevere in the seventies.

Ciao Ciao Disco
97 North 10th Street, Williamsburg, Brooklyn

1:30 A.M.

Before heading back into Manhattan, head to any of the late-night food trucks that hang out up and down Bedford Avenue. You'll find trucks slinging tacos, halal chicken over rice, and Caribbean cuisine. Look for a truck with a few people waiting, and a bunch of happy, drunk customers. It doesn't matter so much what you order, just that you experience the joy of standing on the street, wolfing down your meal, sharing this experience with a bunch of strangers.

3:00 A.M.

Take the L (or grab a cab) into the city to **Marie's Crisis Café**, where you can sing your way into the morning. This show tunes sing-along piano bar is a haven for queer locals, Broadway fans, and sometimes Broadway performers, who pack into the basement bar every night until closing at four A.M. Get your liquid courage from the cheap well drinks and make sure to tip well.

Marie's Crisis Café
59 Grove Street, West Village, Manhattan

4:30 A.M.

Walk west to the Meatpacking District as the sun begins to rise. There you'll find the quintessential diner experience at **Hector's Cafe & Diner** (page 13) which is open twenty-four hours on weekends and and at 5:00 a.m. on weekdays. Hector's has been a solid spot for a cup of strong coffee and a simple meal since 1949, back when the Meatpacking District was more aptly named. Unlike some diners that trade in nostalgia, Hector's is not a monument to Old New York preserved in amber. This is still a working diner, where everyone, from longtime locals to people hitting the clubs to tourist families to, yes, meatpacking workers, comes to order a killer cheeseburger, a breakfast egg platter, or a burrito. And plenty of coffee. Cross over from night-owl to early-bird territory here as you wait for the rest of the city to wake up.

Hector's Cafe & Diner
44 Little West 12th Street, Meatpacking District, Manhattan

7:00 A.M.

By now the High Line will finally be open. In 2009, the city opened the first section of this public park on abandoned former tracks of the New York Central Railroad. Now the park winds from Gansevoort Street to Hudson Yards, with plants inspired by the native brush that grew up through the old tracks, art installations, rolling benches, overlooks, and more. Its creation has spurred debate about gentrification in the area, but there's no doubt it makes for a beautiful, meandering walk.

If you want to extend into the next day . . .
9:00 A.M.

Jump on the B train and head to Brighton Beach in Brooklyn. There you'll find **Tashkent**, a halal supermarket specializing in Uzbek and other Central Asian food. The hot buffet is two lanes long, filled with Afghan plov, pumpkin manti, samsa pastries, and airy norin noodles. Fill up a clamshell with anything and everything and head to the beach, where you can eat your breakfast bounty on a bench on the boardwalk, or if you've brought a towel, enjoy it closer to the surf. From the beach, you can make your way toward Coney Island down the boardwalk. You'll pass the New York Aquarium before you get to the amusement park, featuring historic rides like the Cyclone and Deno's Wonder Wheel. The guys who fish off the Coney Island pier are also basically a landmark.

Tashkent
713 Brighton Beach Avenue, Brighton Beach, Brooklyn

11:00 A.M.
Grab a **Nathan's Famous** (page 155) hot dog for the road and head north to Sunset Park. If you're not ready for lunch yet, take a walk through Green-Wood Cemetery, whose acres upon acres of rolling hills and century-old trees house "permanent residents" like Leonard Bernstein, Jean-Michel Basquiat, and Charles Feltman (inventor of the hot dog). You can also climb to the highest natural elevation in Brooklyn and get a great look at the Manhattan skyline over the mausoleums.

Nathan's Famous
1310 Surf Avenue, Coney Island, Brooklyn

12:30 P.M.
Sunset Park has a massive Latin American population, and the neighborhood is filled with amazing Mexican, Guatemalan, and Salvadorian restaurants. After you've worked up an appetite, walk down to **Don Pepe Tortas y Jugos**. Against one wall are dozens of signs for every possible combination of fresh juices, smoothies, and milkshakes. Against another, even more signs for their famously stuffed tortas, with ingredients like suadero, head cheese, poblano peppers, and arabe pork piled together with vegetables, cheese, and refried beans. Pick something from each wall and eat at the few tables in the back, or two blocks down on a bench in the neighborhood's titular park.

Don Pepe Tortas y Jugos
3908 5th Avenue, Sunset Park, Brooklyn

1:30 P.M.
Walk toward the water to Industry City, a "creative hub" of restaurants, breweries, markets, and businesses in a collection of industrial buildings. There's everything from Jamaican stew from **Reggae Town Cafe**, to Korean kimbap at **Ejen**, to craft beer from **Big aLICe Brewing**, as well as shops selling comic books, vinyl, and bespoke lingerie. Take it all in, then grab a snack or a drink and chill out in one of the many courtyards.

Industry City
220 36th Street, Sunset Park, Brooklyn

3:00 P.M.

Digest on your way back to Manhattan, where you can spend some time wandering through Central Park, because you really can't go wrong with an afternoon in Central Park. Check out the famous carousel, the Bethesda Fountain, and the statue of Alice in Wonderland, and when you start to feel peckish, head over to **William Greenberg Desserts** (page 91). The bakery is known for its kosher pastries, specifically its black-and-white cookies, an NYC staple. You'll be a block away from the Metropolitan Museum of Art, so eat on the steps and pretend you're Gossip Girl.

5:30 P.M.

Continue east to Carl Schurz Park, a lovely slice of riverside greenery that also houses Gracie Mansion, aka the mayor's house. At the top of the park is a ferry terminal that will take you across the river to Astoria, Queens, one of the city's best eating neighborhoods (just kidding—they're all the best). Admire the lighthouse on the tip of Roosevelt Island on your way. Once in Astoria, walk down to Socrates Sculpture Park, which features rotating sculpture installations among the greenery.

6:30 P.M.

When it's time for dinner, go to **Astoria Seafood** (page 105), an institution that's part fish market, part restaurant. Put your name on the list, and once you're in, head to the fish displays to choose which fish and shellfish you want and how you want them cooked. Order the fried calamari, or a whole grilled branzino, but obviously see what looks fresh that day. Make sure to add traditional Greek sides like feta salad, lemon potatoes, and spanakopita, and to BYOB. Another dinner option is **King of Falafel & Shawarma**, a Palestinian falafel and shawarma joint that originated as a street cart in the neighborhood in 2002 and became so popular it allowed them to open a brick-and-mortar shop.

Of course, they're known for their perfectly spiced and crispy falafel, but their chicken over rice is some of the best around.

King of Falafel & Shawarma
30-15 Broadway, Astoria, Queens

9:30 P.M.

An unspoken rule in New York is you should always take an opportunity to do something with a great view. **Anable Basin Sailing** is an unfussy outdoor bar right on the river in Long Island City, serving beer, cocktails, and sausages from a sparse counter. Have a drink, and maybe some cevapi if you're still hungry, while looking at the Manhattan skyline and the boats sailing past.

Anable Basin Sailing
4-40 44th Drive, Long Island City, Queens

11:00 P.M.

For a final nightcap, head away from the shore to **Dutch Kills**, one of the stalwarts of New York's speakeasy trend. The door now shouts the name of the bar in loud colors, and the wooden interior and well-curated jukebox make it the perfect place for any of their impeccably made cocktails, whether it's one of their inventive seasonal offerings or an always-perfect classic daiquiri. Be sure to note the doorknobs on the bathroom doors, which used to be the knobs in all of the city's public schools.

Dutch Kills
27-24 Jackson Avenue, Long Island City, Queens

NYC FOOD CALENDAR

It's never a bad time to dine in New York City, but savvy visitors may want to time a trip to one of the following seasonal events and holidays.

Bastille Day on Smith Street, Brooklyn

Every July 14, the restaurant Bar Tabac takes over a large swath of Smith Street in Brooklyn to celebrate the French holiday Bastille Day. Participants dine on French food at tables in the middle of the street, listen to live music from local bands, and compete in Pétanque tournaments in custom-built sand courts spanning four city blocks.

Bryant Park Movie Nights

The best picnic in New York takes place on Monday nights in the summer in Bryant Park, where New Yorkers crowd the lawn to watch movie screenings with BYO snacks, dinner, and wine.

Feast of San Gennaro, Little Italy

This weeklong festival and street fair, complete with games, shopping, and delicious sausages, cannolis, meatballs, and more, completely subsumes the blocks of Little Italy in Manhattan every September.

Holiday Markets

The holiday season is one of the best times to come to New York. And while the tree at Rockefeller Center gets most of the attention, don't overlook the shopping opportunities at holiday markets in Union Square and Bryant Park. Both feature crafts from local artisans, holiday decor, and festive snacks and drinks.

New York City Wine & Food Festival

Every October, the Food Network throws a weekend-long festival of food events, including dinners, tastings, classes, parties, and panels. The network's big-name stars cameo at most of the festivities alongside local chefs and personalities.

Open Streets

More than 160 locations covering 300 blocks across New York's five boroughs close to car traffic in the warmer months and transform into public spaces, many with games, art, and outdoor dining. The weekend Open Streets programs on Brooklyn's Vanderbilt and Fifth Avenues (running from April through October) are especially vibrant, and great for families.

Queens Night Market

One hundred food and art vendors convene outdoors in Flushing Meadows Corona Park for an eclectic evening of music, eating, and fun on Saturday nights, spring through fall.

Restaurant Week

Twice a year for weeks at a time, hundreds of restaurants across the city offer discounted prix fixe menus for lunch and dinner. Even high-end restaurants participate, so it's a great way to sample bucket-list spots that wouldn't normally be in budget.

Smorgasburg and Brooklyn Flea

Vendors from across the city vie to get a booth at vibrant outdoor Williamsburg food destination Smorgasburg and its more retail-focused sister, Brooklyn Flea (page 159). Both are generally open April through October, and just as acclaimed for the food as they are for the people-watching.

West Indian Day Parade, Crown Heights, Brooklyn

The vibrant, joyous, and delicious celebration that is the West Indian Day Parade takes place in Crown Heights, Brooklyn, on the first Monday of September and features music, dancing, and costumes galore. Most importantly, it features foods from Caribbean island and mainland nations including jerk chicken, curry goat, butterfly shrimp, oxtail, and sugarcane juice.

Bushwick
Greenpoint
Williamsburg

BROO

6

NORTH
OKLYN

NORTH BROOKLYN

DINING

1. Achilles Heel
2. Bamonte's
3. Bernie's
4. Birds of a Feather
5. Bonnie's
6. Bunna Cafe
7. The Commodore
8. Di An Di
9. Diner
10. Falansai
11. The Four Horsemen
12. Frankel's Delicatessen & Appetizing
13. Greenpoint Fish & Lobster Co.
14. Karczma
15. Le Crocodile
16. Leo
17. Lilia
18. Llama Inn
19. Maison Premiere
20. Oasis
21. Oxomoco
22. Peter Luger Steak House
23. Peter Pan Donut & Pastry Shop
24. Pies 'n' Thighs
25. Roberta's
26. Santa Ana Deli & Grocery
27. St. Anselm
28. Taqueria Ramirez
29. Wenwen
30. Win Son

SHOPPING

1. Archestratus Books + Foods
2. Beam
3. Bellocq
4. Big Night
5. Edy's Grocer
6. Fine & Raw Chocolate
7. Foster Sundry
8. Heatonist
9. The Meat Hook
10. Mociun
11. Yun Hai Shop

FRANKLIN ST.

Williamsburg

KENT AVE.

WYTHE AVE.

BERRY ST.

BEDFORD AVE.

METROPOLITAN AVE.

N 7TH ST.

N 6TH ST.

S 6TH ST.

Brooklyn Navy Yard

NORTH BROOKLYN
DINING

When people outside New York talk about Brooklyn, they're likely talking about Williamsburg. The neighborhood, linked to Manhattan's Lower East Side by the bridge that shares its name, is international shorthand for artisanal, craft, hipster, etc. The location of pop-culture hits like *Girls* and *Broad City*, it was before that home to struggling artists and, before that, waves of immigrants. Hasidic Jews, Puerto Ricans, Dominicans, Italians, and Poles carved out neighborhoods within the neighborhoods, including Greenpoint, Bushwick, Williamsburg, that now make up North Brooklyn.

Not surprisingly, then, it's always been home to great food, and lots of it. The restaurateur who arguably kicked off the area's contemporary restaurant boom was Andrew Tarlow, opening Diner in 1999 before launching a full-fledged Brooklyn restaurant empire. It's still there, and shares a block with another of his restaurants, Marlow & Sons, as well as his fancy pantry shop, Marlow & Daughters, a perfect place to grab sandwiches before walking just a couple of blocks to the water to take in idyllic views of Manhattan. A relic of the neighborhood's Industrial Age, the Domino Sugar Refinery (now luxury apartments) towers over Williamsburg's shores. Inland, there's McCarren Park, home to its bustling farmers' market, and between the two, legions of restaurants to choose from.

On the other side of the park is Greenpoint, a harder-to-reach and therefore more relaxing neighborhood, still featuring pierogi and signs in Polish. This residential, park-filled area offers fewer chains and more vintage shops, independent bookstores, and specialty stores. East Williamsburg is where you'll find authentic red-sauce joints and some of the best Puerto Rican restaurants in the city.

If you're spending the day in North Brooklyn, you'll want to end it in Bushwick. These days, Bushwick no longer has the same cartoonish image as a haven for industrial artist lofts and graffiti, as rents are indeed rising, and more money—and by extension fancier establishments—has flooded in. But it remains a hub for nightlife, with venues like House of Yes, affordable late-night dining, a mecca of LGBTQ+ bars, and some of the city's best tacos—thanks to a sizable Latin American community—best eaten during late-night drunchies.

1. Achilles Heel
180 West Street,
Greenpoint

In the winter, Achilles Heel is incredibly cozy, outfitted with a fireplace, a rare find in this city. In the summer, customers spill out onto the West Street corner, watching the sunset and gabbing over glasses of natural wine. Though Achilles Heel is technically a bar, it's also one of the area's best date-night restaurants. Daily-changing shared plates are simple in nature—think cultured butter with bread from Andrew Tarlow's bakery, She Wolf; burrata and bay leaf oil; and ham with melon and chile oil—and highlight the bounty of local produce. Tucked away from the main Greenpoint drag, Achilles Heel feels like a clandestine locals' spot.

2. Bamonte's
32 Withers Street,
Williamsburg

Bamonte's is one of the city's oldest Italian restaurants, having opened its doors in 1900, and continues to stand the test of time. Its antique-filled dining room with red velvet curtains consistently serves up Italian American staples like eggplant rollatini, clams oreganata, chicken parmesan, and cheese ravioli (shown above).

3. Bernie's
332 Driggs Avenue,
Greenpoint

Bernie's is Brooklyn's answer to TGI Fridays: red-and-white checkerboard tablecloths, stained-glass light fixtures, and white paper place mats that invite crayons. Start off with Caesar salad and mozzarella sticks and chase with heaping portions of chicken piccata or a cheeseburger—with an icy martini in hand, of course. Leave room for the maraschino cherry–topped ice cream sundae.

4. Birds of a Feather
191 Grand Street,
Williamsburg

In 2017, Xian Zhang and Yiming Wang, the team behind Midtown hit Café China (page 69), opened this Sichuan spot to much acclaim. Here, find mouth-numbing dishes like the bang bang chicken and spicy cumin lamb. The light-wood dining room, with its elegant accents of porcelain bowls, warm-light-casting lampshades, and lace decals, make the space feel like a serene home.

5. Bonnie's
398 Manhattan Avenue,
Williamsburg

At the James Beard–nominated Bonnie's, find modern spins on Cantonese American cooking nodding to the Brooklyn-born-and-raised chef Calvin Eng's roots. (The restaurant is aptly named after his mother.) Wontons, fuyu cacio e pepe, and the shrimp with candied walnuts are the move here. If you're looking for a restaurant that feels like a party, this is it—sit at the lazy Susan group table and order Long Island iced teas served in teapots.

6. Bunna Cafe

1084 Flushing Avenue,
Williamsburg

This Ethiopian staple is a haven for those looking for a nourishing, colorful, meat-free dining option. Large-format dishes of stewed lentils or beets are served on injera, the spongy Ethiopian bread (shown above), at this low-key spot. Chase your meal with a cup of Ethiopian coffee before heading to the bars or clubs nearby.

7. The Commodore

366 Metropolitan Avenue,
Williamsburg

The Commodore is consistently one of the area's most fun bars. The nautical-themed watering hole serves tropical umbrella-topped frozen drinks among beach chairs, fishing gear, and pinball machines. It also boasts some of the city's best bar food, including fried chicken sandwiches with pickles, shrimp po' boys, and pulled pork barbecue.

8. Di An Di

68 Greenpoint Avenue,
Greenpoint

This gorgeously designed restaurant is dripping in plants and light, with plenty of room for groups. Dishes here showcase a modern take on Vietnamese classics like pork skewers with lemongrass dipping sauce, pho with mushrooms and egg yolk, and pickled radish rice cake omelets. There are lots of vegetarian options, too.

9. Diner

85 Broadway,
Williamsburg

You could spend a whole day in Andrew Tarlow's universe—dinner at restaurant Marlow & Sons, groceries and lunch at butcher shop Marlow & Daughters, drinks at bar Achilles Heel (page 129), and bottles at Stranger Wines & Spirits. But Diner is where it all started, and inside this ninety-year-old dining car you can't go wrong with a martini and whatever daily-changing farm-to-table special is on offer.

10. Falansai

112 Harrison Place,
Williamsburg

Falansai is one of the city's most exciting Vietnamese Mexican restaurants, but it is also one of the best tasting-menu deals in town. Chef and owner Eric Tran offers an ever-changing menu of spicy, experimental, and sometimes offaly dishes at an incredible value. Falansai and its lovely green patio offer a more grown-up experience in a generally younger, nightlife-driven neighborhood.

11. The Four Horsemen

295 Grand Street,
Williamsburg

This Williamsburg restaurant and James Beard Award winner changes its menu daily and consistently offers a banging wine program. It's not inexpensive, but it's not at all pretentious, and it is owned by LCD Soundsystem's James Murphy. If you go for dinner, head next door afterward to Nightmoves, an adjacent but somewhat-hidden nightclub where you can sip on a glass of chilled red and groove on a light-up dance floor.

12. Frankel's Delicatessen & Appetizing

631 Manhattan Avenue, Greenpoint

Frankel's offers a look at the next generation of bakeries. Outfitted to look like a modern-day Brooklyn Russ & Daughters (page 44), Frankel's is all about packaging the best of classic New York ingredients into pillowy bagel sandwiches: Try the pastrami salmon or the lox, cream cheese, and beets. Expect to wait.

13. Greenpoint Fish & Lobster Co.

114 Nassau Avenue, Greenpoint

One of the city's best fish markets, run by a fifth-generation fishmonger, also doubles as a restaurant. New Yorkers order the day's catch to cook at home, but visitors can sit down and order from a menu of lobster rolls, tuna burgers, or the full raw bar.

14. Karczma

136 Greenpoint Avenue, Greenpoint

Greenpoint's Polish roots are best explored at Karczma, a rustic dark-wood stalwart untouched by time. Karczma, meaning "tavern" in Polish, is a go-to for affordable classics like pierogi, white borscht served in a bread bowl, or kielbasa with sautéed cabbage. Enjoy with a chalice of beer and vinegary sides like beet or carrot salad to cut the richness.

15. Le Crocodile

80 Wythe Avenue, Williamsburg

This modern-day French brasserie comes from Aidan O'Neal and Jake Leiber, the duo behind nearby brunch favorite Chez Ma Tante. Conveniently located inside the Wythe Hotel, Le Crocodile serves French onion soup, roasted chicken with fries, and sticky banana date pudding in a romantic atmosphere. After dinner, pop upstairs for drinks at the rooftop Bar Blondeau, where you'll be rewarded with sweeping skyline views of the city.

16. Leo

123 Havemeyer Street, Williamsburg

While Joey Scalabrino and Mike Fadem's pizzeria Ops in Bushwick is a perennial Eater favorite, its sibling spot, Leo, spotlights all things sourdough in more central Williamsburg. Try the clam pizza and chopped Italian salad with a glass of natural wine before indulging in some of the city's best soft serve (flavors rotate based on the season). Order takeout—slices, bottles of wine, cute merch—next door. On the weekends, they sell their own bagels.

17. Lilia

567 Union Avenue, Williamsburg

Chef Missy Robbins's Lilia is by far one of Williamsburg's most talked-about restaurants, known for sensational handmade pasta, including its mafaldine noodles with pink peppercorns. Celebrities like Kim Kardashian and members of the band Haim have flocked to the elegant dining room, refurbished from an old auto-body shop. Reservations are a must. If you can't get one, try your luck at nearby Misi (page 116), its equally buzzy sister pasta spot.

18. Llama Inn

50 Withers Street, Williamsburg

Since opening in 2015, chef Erik Ramirez has ushered in a new era of Peruvian cooking at his Michelin-starred Llama Inn. A rotating menu of dishes and cocktails pulls from a South American palate, with a price point that lends itself to a special occasion. This airy, plant-filled restaurant, nestled under the bustling BQE, is a respite after a long day walking around the area.

19. Maison Premiere
298 Bedford Avenue,
Williamsburg

One of North Brooklyn's sexiest spots by far is New Orleans–style Maison Premiere, outfitted with an ivy-cloaked back area that feels very *Secret Garden*. While nearby cocktail spots can feel like a price gouge, the atmosphere and expertly prepared drinks—there's an absinthe fountain—make Maison Premiere worth it. A raw bar, caviar service, and a variety of crudo round out the opulence.

20. Oasis
168 Bedford Avenue,
Williamsburg

This Williamsburg classic was founded two decades ago by local Palestinian residents who vastly improved the neighborhood's falafel offerings. Now in bigger digs, Oasis has expanded its menu to include chicken and lamb shawarma, the bread salad called fattoush, flaky hand pies, and mousakah, in addition to all of the luscious mezze from the original location.

21. Oxomoco
128 Greenpoint Avenue,
Greenpoint

Oxomoco, on bustling Greenpoint Avenue, ushered in the borough's modern, high-end Mexican moment. This plant-filled restaurant serves an oft-changing menu of dishes like pea shoot tetelas, beet "chorizo" tacos, and beef tartare tostadas with grasshopper mayo. The kitchen, led by Justin Bazdarich (of Speedy Romeo and Bar Tulix), places special emphasis on vegetarian-friendly dishes.

22. Peter Luger Steak House
178 Broadway,
Williamsburg

Every New Yorker has an opinion on the beloved Peter Luger: Whether or not the steak house—open since 1887 in South Williamsburg—has the city's best cut of meat might be debatable, but it's beside the point. This iconic tavern serves up old-school charm with steak house classics, making it a must-visit. Chocolate gold coins come with the check for an extra treat.

23. Peter Pan Donut & Pastry Shop
727 Manhattan Avenue,
Greenpoint

This donut shop, open since the 1950s, is a Greenpoint icon, beloved across the city (and beyond, thanks to its *Spider-Man* cameo). Employees in mint-green-and-pink uniforms serve old-fashioned sour cream or blueberry buttermilk donuts; locals love the $5 breakfast sandwiches served on flagels (flat bagels). Note they don't accept credit cards.

24. Pies 'n' Thighs
166 South 4th Street,
Williamsburg

For nearly two decades, Sarah Sanneh and Carolyn Bane, formerly of Diner (page 130), have served up Southern charm in this dining room made to look like a diner. Not surprisingly, pies and chicken are the thing here—go for banana cream for the former, and choose from a cutlet with biscuits and hot sauce, a sandwich with ranch, bacon, and avocado, or a platter with hush puppies and smoked pork collards for the latter.

25. Roberta's
261 Moore Street,
Bushwick

When Roberta's opened in 2008, it was instrumental in defining Bushwick's food scene, as well as the modern-day pizzeria. These days, Roberta's is sort of an independent chain, with locations on the West Coast and pizzas in the frozen-food aisle, but the original remains a worthy destination. Wood-fired pies like the Bee Sting (with hot honey and soppressata) are the restaurant's calling card and can be ordered in the full-service dining room. They can also be ordered next door, from their take-out location, and eaten in the sprawling backyard with frozen drinks from their outdoor tiki bar.

26. Santa Ana Deli & Grocery

171 Irving Avenue, Bushwick

One of New York City's most essential Mexican spots is actually a bodega that high-lights food from the state of Puebla. A stencil-drawn menu notes dishes like tacos arabes, served in flour tortillas. Eater critic Robert Sietsema considers this affordable spot one of his all-time favorites for tacos in New York City, best washed down with a glass bottle of fruity Jarritos.

27. St. Anselm

355 Metropolitan Avenue, Williamsburg

This Williamsburg steak house has casual, wood-paneled interiors and well-priced entrees—and you do not have to dress up for dinner. Dishes like lamb chop served with salsa verde, sweet tea–brined chicken, and skate wings with a caper sauce offer a little zhuzh-up to the steak house concept.

28. Taqueria Ramirez

94 Franklin Street, Greenpoint

New York's not a town known for its tacos, but Taqueria Ramirez is chang-ing that. Once you wait in the long line (it's best to go off-hours), you'll find incredible tacos filled with offbeat meat cuts, like the suadero (thick cuts of beef stewed for hours in a choricera, a cauldron of sorts typical in Mexico City), lesser seen on Brooklyn menus. Seats are limited—there are just a handful inside—but on a sunny day, there's no better North Brooklyn play than perching outside on the bench with a colorful plate crowded with tacos and watching the people stroll by.

29. Wenwen

1025 Manhattan Avenue, Greenpoint

Eric Sze, behind the East Village Taiwanese spot 886, opened this larger, more mature Brooklyn sibling where the food is just as good, if not better. Taiwanese Old-Fashioneds are best paired with chick-pea noodles, celtuce salad, and popcorn chicken, an equally worthy dupe for the limited-supply "BDSM"—aka brined, deboned, soy-milk-battered—chicken. Don't skip the extremely savory black sesame tangyuan dessert with cilantro.

30. Win Son

159 Graham Avenue, Williamsburg

Win Son was at the fore-front of Brooklyn's wave of Taiwanese American restaurants. Its menu, including lu rou fan (a rice dish with minced pork and a soy egg), sloppy baos (with pork and peanuts), and a tofu version of fly's head, packs plenty of swagger and is served inside an understated-but-cool room. Across the street you'll find Win Son Bakery, where you can order mochi donuts and red date cake starting at nine A.M.

QR CODES for our online guides to NORTH BROOKLYN neighborhoods:

BUSHWICK

GREENPOINT

WILLIAMSBURG

NORTH BROOKLYN
SHOPPING

North Brooklyn has been shaped by the steady stream of youth that has flocked to the neighborhood since the early aughts, beginning with artists and musicians, and evolving to include New York transplants looking for the version of Brooklyn that those initial creatives helped define. Businesses in the area reflect these shifts. The twenty-first century has seen the area become a hub for vintage and thrift stores and shops showcasing the handiwork of local artisans. Even more recently, fancy food shops and high-end butchers have made North Brooklyn home, catering to a trend-conscious crowd that understands that food—as much as art and music—is now an essential part of popular culture.

1. Archestratus Books + Foods

160 Huron Street, Greenpoint

Since 2015, Archestratus has become a community hub for Brooklyn food lovers. The shop sells both vintage and new cookbooks, plus other books and gifts with a food focus, while a café serves coffee and Sicilian baked goods (don't skip the rainbow cookies). Check the schedule for events with just as much variety, from book clubs and release parties to classes on how to make those famous rainbow cookies.

2. Beam

272 Kent Avenue, Williamsburg

Broadly, Beam is a home decor store, with a full selection of furniture and smaller items for every room. But the kitchen section in particular is worth a visit for the statement-making glassware and ceramics. Beam describes its style as "a little bit mid-century, a little bit rock-and-roll; a Southern California meets Brooklyn mashup." We'd add to that list of dichotomies: prices at both the low and high ends of the spectrum.

3. Bellocq

104 West Street, Greenpoint

Bellocq's blink-and-you'll-miss-it Greenpoint storefront is part of its charm. The luxury tea brand's plant-filled space—which it refers to as its atelier—transports its visitors to an oasis of calm. Once inside, you'll find beautifully packaged loose-leaf teas and tea blends, made on-site, tea accessories to satisfy a range of aesthetic preferences, and, of course, the option to enjoy a cup as you shop.

4. Big Night

154 Franklin Street, Greenpoint

Big Night is all about the dinner party. Whether you need a new set of glasses or the evening's appetizer course, this small Greenpoint storefront has you covered. With brands known for having an equal stake in both form and function, like Estelle Colored Glass, and internet favorites Fly by Jing and Fishwife, it's also the perfect place to shop for the consummate hosts in your life. It also has a location in the West Village.

5. Edy's Grocer

136 Meserole Avenue, Greenpoint

Edy Massih got his start as a private chef and caterer before opening up this Lebanese deli and market in Greenpoint. Pick up picnic-perfect sandwiches and mezze, or shop for Middle Eastern snacks and a collection of dry goods packaged in-house. After hours, Edy's hosts dinners and events with chefs both locally and from around the country, making it a center for the food community, as well as a grocery store worth a special trip.

6. Fine & Raw Chocolate

70 Scott Avenue, Williamsburg

You may see Fine & Raw chocolates at the counters of many a Brooklyn grocery store, but at the Fine & Raw factory in East Williamsburg you can see how the organic, plant-based bars come to be. There are tours on offer, but simply wandering the brand's café and shop will give you a glimpse into the workings of the factory.

7. Foster Sundry

215 Knickerbocker Avenue, Bushwick

In 2015 Aaron Foster, a Murray's Cheese (page 18) vet, opened modern butcher and gourmet grocer Foster Sundry. The awning of Bushwick's Foster Sundry makes clear its multihyphenate status: As the fabric states, it has craft beer, strong coffee, tasty sandwiches, and, perhaps most important to the casual shopper, great snacks. And while the concept—a general store for the epicurean set—is one that tends to pop up frequently in this borough, Foster Sundry has made itself a neighborhood staple for its mastery of the form.

8. Heatonist

121 Wythe Avenue, Williamsburg

Spice fans have flocked to Heatonist for small-batch hot sauces—and nothing else—since 2015. And given this ever-expanding condiment category, a dedicated one-stop hot-sauce shop continues to make total sense. But, more than a store, Heatonist is a tasting room, complete with a hot-sauce sommelier there to help shoppers match up their preferences to a sauce in Heatonist's sizable inventory, which includes the full line of sauces from hit YouTube series *Hot Ones*. To that end, trying before buying is highly encouraged.

9. The Meat Hook
397 Graham Avenue, Williamsburg

The butcher shop in East Williamsburg is worth a visit for anyone interested in thoughtful butchery, as well as fans of the Eater video series *Prime Time* (starring founders Ben Turley and Brent Young). And there's more than meat on offer. Although quality, pasture-raised meat—and supporting the farms that supply it—is the shop's raison d'être, it also sells grocery and pantry items plus Meat Hook–made sauces and merch.

10. Mociun
683 Driggs Avenue, Williamsburg

At this Williamsburg shop, Caitlin Mociun assembles a collection of home goods befitting a sought-after jewelry designer. Alongside Mociun jewels, you'll find eye-catching vases, glassware, and the most giftable mugs. Compared to the diamonds they share space with, they're a bargain, though they feel just as special.

11. Yun Hai Shop
170 Montrose Avenue, Williamsburg

In 2022, online shop Yun Hai opened its first brick-and-mortar in Williamsburg. The same artisan-sourced products that made the site a destination for Taiwanese pantry staples are now available to peruse in real life, including the Su Chili Crisp (the line of small-batch chili crisps that essentially launched the site), dried fruit, and an admirable selection of soy sauces.

BEYOND RESTAURANTS

Coffee Shops
Brooklyn Ball Factory
Devoción
Partners Coffee
Qahwah House
Sey Coffee

Bars
320 Club
Bar Blondeau
Lucky Dog
Maracuja
Masquerade
Palmetto
Sauced
Skinny Dennis
Union Pool

Bakeries
Ceremonia Bakeshop
L'imprimerie
Ovenly
Radio Bakery
Roberta's Bakery
Win Son Bakery

Ice Cream/Sweets
Taiyaki NYC
Uncle Louie G
Van Leeuwen Ice Cream

THREE NEW YORKER– APPROVED OVERNIGHT TRIPS

By Erika Adams

If you're in town for a longer time, consider an overnight or weekend trip to Long Island or Upstate, areas beloved by locals and filled to the brim with great dining, shopping, and activities.

Day Trip 1: The North Fork,
by Phillip Lim

Phillip Lim is the cofounder and creative director of 3.1 Phillip Lim, an award-winning fashion brand based in NYC. He's been a New Yorker for about twenty years and, in that time, has gotten to know the city's restaurant scene very well. But when everything came to a halt during the pandemic, he started cooking up another side project: More Than Our Bellies, a collection of recipes, marketplace, and online community that Lim founded to celebrate food and togetherness during lockdown.

One of his favorite places to day-trip outside New York City—and where he can be found filming cooking videos for More Than Our Bellies on TikTok and Instagram— is Long Island's North Fork, or what he fondly calls "the antithesis of the Hamptons." The island splits into two prongs at its farthest reaches; the Hamptons are located to the south, while the North Fork, dotted with vineyards and farmland, stretches out to the north. It's a quieter area, he says, where you're more apt to run into a resident than a fellow tourist. "You're surrounded by water, and it has the most beautiful sunsets," Lim says. As for the food? "It really defines the idea of farm to table, literally."

Check out Lim's top picks for dining, shopping, and more in the North Fork:

Where to stay
Sound View Greenport
58775 County Road 48, Greenport
I would check in at Sound View, which is kind of a charming renovated seaside motel. I'd stay there because it's central to all the hamlets, but it also looks out onto Long Island Sound, which has the most stunning views. Long Island Sound is also a place where the water is calm enough that you can go paddleboarding or kayaking, or take a walk along the beach. There's tons of local neighborhood beaches all around.

For breakfast

Main Road Biscuit Co.

1601 Main Road, Jamesport

It sells exactly what the name suggests: great homemade biscuits. It's the best place to get chicken and waffles, or chicken and biscuits. They usually sell out of their biscuits in the morning.

Where the locals grab coffee

North Fork Roasting Co.

55795 Main Road, Southold

Imagine Central Perk on *Friends*, but North Fork style. There's a living room, a sofa, and a chocolate Lab running around.

For fancy baked goods

Southold General

54180 Main Road, Southold

This is on Main Street in the hamlet of Southold, and it's run by a famous French pastry chef, François Payard. It's the place where you can get coffee, amazing sandwiches, the best salads, and incredible sourdough bread. A bit more upscale, but it's really good.

For vintage shopping in an old church

Beall & Bell

430 Main Street, Greenport

It's amazing. It's basically a vintage furniture shop housed in an old Masonic temple. The curation is incredible because it's really beautiful pieces, but they're not expensive. Everything has a beautiful, aged patina but with a very masterful, curated eye from the proprietors. I always love to go in there because it's so inspiring when you walk into an empty church full of just beautiful antique and vintage furniture that is affordable. It's super friendly, and it won't break the bank.

For lunch

Orient Country Store

950 Village Lane, Orient

I would rent a bicycle—it's so beautiful to ride bikes along the Fork—and I would just ride it all the way to Orient, which is at the tip of Long Island Sound along the North Fork. I would have lunch at the Orient Country Store, which is run by Miriam and her family. It's a local bodega, but it's not only a bodega; it's also a place where you can buy classic American sandwiches and soups, and you can leave a tab there. They make the best Reubens and roast beef melts and carrot-ginger soups, and they also have delicious baked goods. It's so charming, and they are so kind there. Please say hello and tell them that Phillip sent you.

Afternoon activity

Touring North Fork's vineyards and farms

There are thirty-seven vineyards on this Fork. It's basically Long Island wine country. And in between the vineyards are farms and farm stands. After that delicious lunch, take that bike, go on the wine trails, do wine tastings. Then, I would stop by Lavender by the Bay, which is a little lavender farm in the middle of the Fork. People go there just to sit

in the middle of lavender fields. You can pick your own lavender, you can buy bushels, you can buy lavender soap, lotion—anything you can imagine that lavender can be in, you can find there.

For cocktails and dinner

The Halyard
58775 County Road 48, Greenport
I would do cocktails and dinner at the Halyard, a very good restaurant at the Sound View hotel. They have beautiful cocktails, and the space overlooks the sunset. And you've been out all day already, so, you know, it's time to just be present in your surroundings.

Nighttime activity

Stargazing
The North Fork is amazing not only for agriculture, but also for nature hikes and stargazing, because it's an area that has light pollution restrictions. I was there last night, and it was dreamy. You're like, *Wow, the stars, where am I?* And it's only about an hour and a half away from New York City.

Day Trip 2: Montauk,
by Maangchi

A New York City resident since 2008, Emily Kim is a Korean cooking star who is better known as Maangchi to her millions of online followers. Fans flock to her YouTube videos and accompanying website, which she has run for the past fifteen years, to find a vast collection of recipes, straightforward how-to cooking guides, and two published cookbooks that showcase Korean home cooking. Some of her most popular cooking videos, like a step-by-step guide to making traditional kimchi, have racked up twenty-five million views and counting.

When Maangchi needs a break from Manhattan, she heads to Montauk, at the very tip of Long Island's South Fork. "I can get there easily from Manhattan by train, and I can stay right on the beach and cook and eat fresh seafood," she says. The oceanfront setting reminds her of her childhood home—South Korea's port city of Yeosu—and the fish market's daily seafood catch is worth the morning wait from shore. Sometimes, her haul will spark inspiration for cooking videos: Maangchi has filmed herself making nongeo-maeuntang, or spicy fish stew with sea bass, and saeu-juk, a savory shrimp porridge.

Follow along with Maangchi for where to stay, what to eat, and where to find the best seafood in Montauk:

Where to stay
Condo at the Surf Club at Montauk
20 Surfside Avenue, Montauk

I stay at the Surf Club because of the oceanfront. I can see the ocean rise from my bedroom. I can hear the sound of the waves, and I love that because I was born and raised in a harbor city in Korea. All the time, ever since I was young, I've always been familiar with the sound of the waves. So, whenever I go to the Surf Club, I stay in an oceanfront small apartment. I feel like I'm in my hometown. Also, the smell of the sea—the sea breeze. I love it.

For bagels and coffee
Goldberg's Bagels
28 South Etna Avenue, Montauk

I usually make Korean food at home [for breakfast], but not all the time.

I stopped by here in the morning because I ran out of coffee, and people were lining up at this place. The coffee was so good, and also the bagels. [Her favorite bagel order? Cream cheese and salmon.]

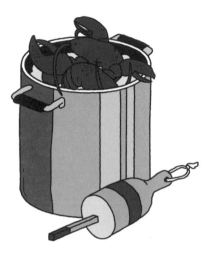

Where to buy seafood off incoming fishing boats

Gosman's Gourmet Fish Market
484 West Lake Drive, Montauk

Without Gosman's, there's no reason to go to Montauk. They do live lobster, scallops, shrimp, salmon, but I need that really freshly caught fish. They open at ten A.M., and I call them like, "Okay, I want to bring [home] some freshly caught fish." And then sometimes I just go there and wait for the fish. [Last time Maangchi visited, she bought a fresh five-pound fluke off an incoming fishing

boat.] They asked me, "Do you want me to cut it up?" I said, "No, no, no. Just give it to me." I want to do it all by my own methods. I fileted the fish and then divided it so I can make many kinds of dishes.

Where to go while waiting for the fish to arrive

Homeport
85 The Plaza, Montauk

For shopping, I liked this place called Homeport near the fish market. That location closed during the pandemic, but there is another one on the main street [in downtown Montauk], which is great for home goods and kitchenware. It's a very beautiful small store with decorations, plates, and even jewelry. While I'm waiting for my fish, I always look around and buy something.

For non-fish food

Montauk farmers' market

There's a farmers' market right next to IGA [a grocery store in Montauk]. There's eggs and berries and beautiful vegetables; even the lettuce is good quality there. I always shop around there.

Midday activity

Montauk Point Lighthouse

Some people go to Montauk for only one purpose, to see this. There's beautiful scenery; you're surrounded by the Atlantic Ocean. You can walk around there, and there's a sort of snack bar—George's Lighthouse Cafe—where you can get a beverage and a quick kind of meal.

You can get there by train—three and a half hours in the early morning. And then in the same day, you can come back. I thought this was a nice thing for young couples who are dating. They can talk a lot on the train, and then see the ocean. Also, it's cheap!

But just for me, I like the beautiful scenery you can see around there, and to really enjoy the sea breeze.

For live music

668 the Gig Shack
782 Montauk Highway, Montauk

There's live music and it is *very* loud. There're also lots of local people hanging around, listening to the music. It's a nice place to spend time.

For dinner out at a restaurant

South Edison
17 South Edison Street, Montauk

I usually don't eat out when I am there, but I like South Edison for fresh seafood. There's other stuff, but I focus on the seafood. I'm not going to eat the steak there. Montauk is seafood famous!

Day Trip 3: The Hudson Valley,
by Alexander Smalls

Alexander Smalls has lived many lives. The Grammy- and Tony-winning former opera singer is best known now as an acclaimed chef and restaurateur, James Beard Award–winning cookbook author, and occasional cooking show judge—and he has been known to host the best dinner parties in New York City from his Harlem home.

For weekend trips outside the city, Smalls likes to head up north to the Hudson Valley. "I'm very blessed and fortunate to have lots of friends who have homes from the Catskills up to Hudson, New York, and I've spent a lot of time in those areas," Smalls says. "What a great resource of not only farms and farm products but wonderful bakeries and inns with great roaring fireplaces and dining halls. I've always preferred that part of New York. Nothing beats the countryside."

Below, find Smalls's top picks for where to stay, what to eat, and the best place for Sunday dinner in the Hudson Valley.

For breakfast

Cafe Mio
2356 US 44, Gardiner

It's a place that my friend always takes me. It's easy and friendly. To have people who greet you in the day with a smile and generosity and, of course, fresh pastries and breakfast . . . it is my most favorite food of the day. All you have to do is go to my Instagram to see that I'm just obsessed with breakfast. I probably post more breakfast photos than anything. It's the most exciting food. It's colorful and rich and full of textures.

For brunch and lunch and great cocktails

The Amsterdam
6380 Mill Street, Rhinebeck

It looks like a house. It's got a very homey vibe, which I like. The people seem very cheerful there. And they have different ways to eat—small plates, or something big—which is always fun. They have fresh salads, charcuterie, and a whole baked chicken with fries, which I love. The bartender there once made me a mint julep, too. They are very accommodating, and it's a fresh, warm environment.

I've been there with large parties, too, and we've been able to sit all together at a big table. So when you're having multiple friends collect and gather, it's just a fun place.

It almost feels like *Cheers*, you know, where everybody knows your name.

Midday activity

Get a friend who has a boat and go boating, or grill in the backyard

When I'm out boating, I cruise. And I drink the beverages. I have friends in the area who just live on the water. We go out for an afternoon of boating on the Hudson River, and we take the boat up from Rhinebeck to the town of Hudson, where other friends are. I'm so not in charge of the planning. I have no idea how it happens, except friends with boats make it happen.

Now, when it comes to grilling, that's usually me in the backyard at friends' homes. Everybody has a grill. And my barbecue sauce is legendary. [The recipes for various versions of that famous sauce can be found in Smalls's three cookbooks.]

For weekday dinner
Le Petit Bistro
2 East Market Street, Rhinebeck
I just love the name. It reminds me of my years living in Paris as a young opera singer. It definitely has that Parisian feel. It's small, and it's located in Rhinebeck, which is already picturesque to begin with. It's light and airy. They have a *great* oyster bar. That's such a big thing for me. I love, love, love oysters.

At the same time, they have an interesting menu that runs the gamut of the common things you'd expect, like salads and pâtés and smoked salmon, which I live for. I could have a whole meal with oysters and smoked salmon and pâté. I could go heavy on seafood, too: I love seared scallops, things like that. And the dessert ain't shabby, either. They do a fruit brioche with apples or pears. And where can you go and have a pudding? People don't do puddings, and I grew up on Jell-O pudding. I think they have some kind of toffee pudding cake.

They also have nice drinks. They have this lavender sour, and I sometimes substitute the vodka or gin with bourbon. I'm a Southern boy. Any opportunity to do that, I love that.

For Sunday dinner
Stissing House
7801 South Main Street, Pine Plains
It's intimate and cozy, and it has chicken liver pâté, which, you know, I love that. I could do without the radishes, but I *love* the pâté. They also serve trout. There're not always many restaurants that serve trout, and so I love that a lot. They also have a brownie butterscotch sundae. I remember that because that's such a Southern thing. I grew up on butterscotch.

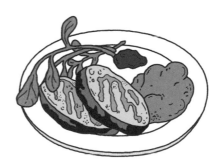

BREAKFAST AND BRUNCH

Skip the hotel breakfast and find New York's standout pancakes, Austrian spreads, Malaysian kaya toast, and Taiwanese soy milk at these breakfast and lunch staples.

Bubby's

120 Hudson Street, Tribeca, Manhattan

A Tribeca icon for a reason, Bubby's is a family-friendly pancake and pie destination that's always bustling, especially on the weekend.

Buvette

42 Grove Street, West Village, Manhattan

The eggs at chef Jody Williams's Grove Street charmer are cooked with the steam wand on the espresso machine, normally used to make a cappuccino—and they're perfect.

Chez Ma Tante

90 Calyer Street, Greenpoint, Brooklyn

For brunch in North Brooklyn, there's no better place than Chez Ma Tante, known for their oversized, fluffy pancakes.

Clinton St. Baking Company

4 Clinton Street, Lower East Side, Manhattan

This place serves the most famous pancakes in the city, as underscored by the long lines of people vying for a stack on any given Sunday.

Davelle

102 Suffolk Street, Lower East Side, Manhattan

This sparse Japanese café serves stylish and photogenic (but also delicious!) breakfast toasts.

Golden Diner

123 Madison Street, Chinatown, Manhattan

Breakfast is served all day, so you can have honey butter pancakes whenever the craving hits (page 36).

Ho Foods

110 East 7th Street, East Village, Manhattan

Choose breakfast from a small menu that includes dishes like homemade soy milk, scallion pancakes with egg, chile wontons, radish cake, garlicky cucumbers, and zha jiang noodles.

Koloman

16 West 29th Street, Nomad, Manhattan

Koloman (page 71), in Nomad's Ace Hotel, offers breakfast and brunch menus that include fluffy croissants and other assorted cakes and pastries made in-house, eggs with meats on the side, and a full Viennese spread.

Kopitiam

151 East Broadway, Lower East Side, Manhattan

The sunny, colorful Malaysian café (page 37) kicks off all-day breakfast service at ten A.M. with dishes like kaya toast, half-boiled eggs with soy sauce and pepper, and fish ball soup.

Okonomi

150 Ainsle Street, Williamsburg, Brooklyn

For an austere and delightful Japanese breakfast, check out this tiny spot on a side street in Williamsburg.

Spanish Diner

10 Hudson Yards, Hudson Yards, Manhattan

Chef José Andrés's Hudson Yards food hall, Mercado Little Spain, is home to a full-service diner that offers a lovely breakfast starting at eleven A.M. daily, or at ten A.M. on weekends.

Thai Diner

186 Mott Street, Nolita, Manhattan

The namesake egg sandwich, served with Thai sausage and wrapped in roti, is a must-order (page 38).

Win Son Bakery

164 Graham Avenue, Williamsburg, Brooklyn

For an exemplary Taiwanese American breakfast, complete with mochi doughnuts, veggie milk buns, and breakfast sandwiches, go to Win Son Bakery for breakfast or Win Son (page 133), its sister restaurant, for weekend brunch.

Bed-Stuy
Brighton Beach
Brooklyn Heights
Brooklyn Navy Yard
Carroll Gardens
Cobble Hill
Coney Island
Crown Heights
Downtown
  Brooklyn
Dumbo

Flatbush
Fort Greene
Gowanus
Gravesend
Midwood
Park Slope
Prospect Heights
Prospect Lefferts
  Gardens
Red Hook
Sunset Park

THE RI
BROO

7

EST OF
OKLYN

THE REST OF BROOKLYN

DINING

1. A&A Bake and Doubles
2. Al Badawi
3. Chuan Tian Xia
4. Court Street Grocers
5. Defonte's
6. Di Fara Pizza
7. Gage & Tollner
8. Gloria's
9. Haenyeo
10. Hart's
11. Hometown Bar-B-Que
12. Insa
13. Kashkar Cafe
14. L&B Spumoni Gardens
15. The Long Island Bar
16. Lucali
17. Miss Ada
18. Nathan's Famous
19. Olmsted
20. Peaches HotHouse
21. Peppa's
22. Purple Yam
23. Red Hook Tavern
24. Syko
25. Tacos El Bronco
26. Tatiana
27. Ugly Baby
28. Ursula
29. Winner
30. Yemen Café

SHOPPING

1. Brooklyn Flea
2. Fermented Grapes
3. Grand Army Plaza Greenmarket
4. Jacques Torres
5. Japan Village at Industry City
6. Kings County Distillery
7. Labay Market
8. Marché Rue Dix
9. Mazzola Bakery
10. Sahadi's
11. Salter House
12. Whisk

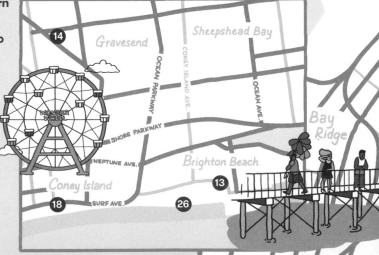

THE REST OF BROOKLYN
DINING

First off, we must acknowledge that it was a Herculean task editing down the rest of Brooklyn into one map; this is meant to be a taste and in no way encompasses all the nuances and multiplicity of cultures that make up Kings County. The rest of Brooklyn may garner less buzz than the north side, but it boasts an explosive food scene. Prospect Heights offers big-time chef-y restaurants alongside casual neighborhood favorites. Not too far away, Cobble Hill and Brooklyn Heights, some of the borough's most expensive neighborhoods, marked by waterfront views, several iconic Middle Eastern grocery stores, and dozens of celebrity-owned homes, make for an ideal daytime stroll and shopping zone. The elevated promenade leads down to industrial Dumbo, where you'll find one of the most photographed streets in the whole country.

Build up an appetite and end up in an area like Carroll Gardens, with its Italian American pizza parlors, pastry shops, and delis. Continue farther afield south and you'll find Sunset Park and Bay Ridge, which brim with restaurants that run the gamut from Chinese to Palestinian, Mexican, and more. And, of course, even farther from Manhattan are Brighton Beach, with its Russian, Georgian, and Ukrainian establishments, and Coney Island, home to Luna Park amusements and boardwalk treats like Nathan's hot dogs. By night, head to Crown Heights (best known for its Caribbean and kosher Jewish spots) and Bed-Stuy (for its soul food and Trinidadian doubles), where there are lively dinner and bar spots, new and old, that reflect a changing neighborhood. In the end, you'll start thinking like a longtime local who says things like, "Oh, I never go into Manhattan anymore."

1. A&A Bake and Doubles

1337 Fulton Street,
Bed-Stuy

This casual counter-service spot specializes in doubles, a specialty in Trinidad, where fried bread is stuffed with a hearty vegetarian chickpea curry called chana, and overstuffed rotis.

2. Al Badawi

151 Atlantic Avenue,
Brooklyn Heights

When Ayat, the fast-casual, halal-friendly Palestinian joint, opened in October 2020 in Bay Ridge, it exploded in popularity, and it has since expanded with a second location called Al Badawi on Atlantic Avenue, as well as several other locations throughout town. The full-service Al Badawi has many of the same dishes that Ayat came to be known for—including kebabs and mansaf (a fermented yogurt-based lamb dish)—and new items like flatbreads with pistachio and fasolia (green beans and beef in a tomato stew).

3. Chuan Tian Xia

5502 7th Avenue,
Sunset Park

Sunset Park has its own Chinatown, teeming with restaurants that in recent years have been run by an influx of immigrants from Fujian Province. One such standout is Chuan Tian Xia, which is owned by a couple from Fujian but serves a Sichuan menu. Sichuan food, a cuisine known for its mouth-numbing Sichuan peppercorns, can be enjoyed through the huge, family-style portions of items like wrapped fish, frog legs, mapo tofu, and tofu with salted egg yolk.

4. Court Street Grocers

485 Court Street,
Carroll Gardens

Sandwich spot Court Street Grocers opened more than a decade ago on Carroll Gardens' Court Street and has since sprouted into a mini-empire, with several additional locations and full-service spin-offs. Known for playful names like the Uncle Chucky (roasted cauliflower with pickled fennel and a sumac vinaigrette), written with handmade signs, there are sandwiches for every time of day and every dietary restriction here. Each Court Street Grocers also doubles as a pantry shop, selling otherwise hard-to-find condiments, snacks, and the company's own line of sodas.

5. Defonte's

379 Columbia Street,
Red Hook

Defonte's, located on an otherwise desolate Red Hook street, is one of Brooklyn's best Italian delis. Behemoth sandwiches have been slammed and stacked together here since 1922. Head here for subs like gabagool, eggplant parm, turkey with gravy, and more combinations that feel untouched by time. Note: It's cash only, and there are no tables here, but there's a small park nearby.

6. Di Fara Pizza

1424 Avenue J,
Midwood

Though Domenico "Dom" DeMarco, the legendary owner behind this Midwood slice shop, open since 1965, passed away in March 2022, the pizzeria continues to serve some of the city's best slices. DeMarco especially established Di Fara as a take-out joint with a slow-food approach, never cutting corners with his high-quality ingredients.

7. Gage & Tollner

372 Fulton Street,
Downtown Brooklyn

The restaurant, which first opened in 1879, was meticulously restored and relaunched in 2021. It gives new life to classic, and some forgotten, American dishes. The menu highlights pork potpie, a raw bar, dry-aged steaks sold by the ounce, and a Baked Alaska for two. Make reservations in advance, and check out the speakeasy-ish nautical cocktail bar upstairs called Sunken Harbor Club before or after the meal.

8. Gloria's
987 Nostrand Avenue,
Crown Heights

Long-time Caribbean restaurant Gloria's serves Trinidadian specialties like curry goat and stewed oxtail roti, with plenty of veggie options like tofu substitutions to boot. It's a bare-bones operation, but Prospect Park is a short walk away if you want to take your meal there.

9. Haenyeo
239 5th Avenue,
Park Slope

Park Slope's culinary scene got turned up a notch when Haenyeo, a modern Korean restaurant, opened its doors. Chef Jenny Kwak gives playful spins to the cuisine with dishes like her popular cheesy and spicy rice cake fundido. Haenyeo is open for dinner and has an impressive cocktail and wine list.

10. Hart's
506 Franklin Avenue,
Bed-Stuy

This tiny but mighty restaurant right below the Franklin Avenue C train platform is one of the area's best date spots. The go-tos here are the lamb burger with anchovies, clam toast, pork Milanese, and other dishes that lean into briny flavors of the Mediterranean. Check out their equally wonderful sister spots the Fly, a cocktail bar serving rotisserie chicken a couple of blocks away, and Cervo's (page 35) on the Lower East Side.

11. Hometown Bar-B-Que
454 Van Brunt Street,
Red Hook

The East Coast may not be as known for its stellar barbecue, but Hometown Bar-B-Que is something special. Located in Red Hook (now also with an additional Industry City outpost), this cavernous, wood-paneled restaurant is worth the trip to one of the more remote neighborhoods in Brooklyn. Platters of this Texas-style barbecue include brisket, pulled pork, corn bread, and all the saucy condiments. It's an easy ride into Manhattan on the ferry after.

12. Insa
328 Douglass Street,
Gowanus

One of the top Korean barbecue spots in Brooklyn also doubles as one of the best places for karaoke in the city. This large restaurant features long tables outfitted with grills on which servers will help you cook galbi, rib eye, or mushroom platters. Banchan—Korean small plates, consisting of various fermented items like kimchi—come, as is typical, complimentary. Cool down with a glass of the sweet alcoholic rice drink makgeolli.

13. Kashkar Cafe
1141 Brighton Beach Avenue,
Brighton Beach

The ornately decorated but casual Kashkar Cafe specializes in Uyghur food, a cuisine from China's Muslim minority. The halal-friendly specialties include the flaky pumpkin-stuffed pastry samsa, lamb manti, and a meat and vegetable noodle dish called lagman.

14. L&B Spumoni Gardens
2725 86th Street,
Gravesend

Gravesend's L&B Spumoni Gardens is known for its hefty, square grandma-style slices, and, of course, as the name suggests, its tricolored spumoni ice cream served in plastic cups. Inside, there's a full-service restaurant that serves red-sauce classics like penne alla vodka, but L&B is definitely more known for its order-at-the-counter offerings.

15. The Long Island Bar
110 Atlantic Avenue,
Cobble Hill

Modeled after an old-school diner, the Long Island Bar is a timeless New York hit with cozy booths and Formica-style tabletops. The owner of the Long Island Bar is credited with creating the cosmopolitan cocktail, so it's a requisite drink order here. Note the full-service establishment is also known in equal measure for its pickle-outfitted burgers and cheese curds that are hearty enough to be considered a full-blown dinner.

16. Lucali

575 Henry Street,
Carroll Gardens

After all these years, it's still worth the crazy lines that, yes, can sometimes be upwards of two hours. Pizzaiolo Mark Iacono has been serving pies—there's just one type, plain, available with toppings like mushroom or pepperoni— for more than a decade in a dining room where guests can see the brick oven. Note: Lucali is BYOB and cash only.

17. Miss Ada

184 Dekalb Avenue,
Fort Greene

Located just a block away from Fort Greene Park in a tree-lined area of the neighborhood, Miss Ada is one of the area's most exciting restaurants. Known for its Middle Eastern cuisine—seen in dishes like beet hummus, chicken shawarma with spices, and shakshuka—this restaurant is a favorite among brunchgoers. Reservations are a must, but if you encounter

a wait as a walk-in, take a stroll in the park to kill time.

18. Nathan's Famous

1310 Surf Avenue,
Coney Island

There's nothing like a hot dog at an amusement park, and there's probably no more iconic way to do it than at Nathan's, open since 1916, in Coney Island. Dollop on some relish and mustard and/or ketchup squiggles and bring it for a walk on the boardwalk, the beach, or even the Luna Park Ferris wheel. Each year on July Fourth, the stalwart holds a beloved and much-attended hot dog–eating contest.

19. Olmsted

659 Vanderbilt Avenue,
Prospect Heights

When Alinea alum Greg Baxtrom opened his whimsical farm-to-table restaurant in sleepier Prospect Heights in 2016, he set forth a new chapter for the neighborhood as a fine-dining destination. He's since followed up with Five Acres in Rockefeller Center and Patti Ann's, a Midwestern-inspired comfort-food joint,

especially well suited for families dining with children.

20. Peaches HotHouse

415 Tompkins Avenue,
Bed-Stuy

With several locations around Brooklyn, Peaches is synonymous with Brooklyn soul food. There are fried catfish sandwiches, fried green tomatoes, fried chicken, and must-have sides like corn bread (shown below). Afterward, head down the street to Lovers Rock or one of the many other bars on the Tompkins Avenue strip, just a short walk away from nearby Herbert Von King Park.

21. Peppa's

738 Flatbush Avenue,
Flatbush

In the Little Caribbean area of Flatbush, jerk chicken favorite Peppa's is a must. While jerk seasonings vary, Gavin Hussey's (aka Peppa's) version differs from his competitors' with a tangy white vinegar wash and then a dry rub of a secret mix of seasonings. Stop by this Jamaican fast-casual neighborhood institution for a true taste of Brooklyn right before seeing a show at the iconic Kings Theatre.

22. Purple Yam
1314 Cortelyou Road,
Flatbush

Though Filipino restaurants are increasingly easier to find in NYC, Purple Yam led the pack when it opened in South Brooklyn in 2009. Owner Romy Dorotan offers dishes like chicken adobo, the national favorite in the Philippines, alongside pork lumpia rolls with a sour pineapple sauce, and the Filipino noodle dish pancit. Purple Yam is a no-frills establishment located on Cortelyou Road, less than a mile from an entrance of Prospect Park.

23. Red Hook Tavern
329 Van Brunt Street,
Red Hook

At Hometown Bar-B-Que (page 154), Billy Durney fires off next-level Texas-style barbecue. At Red Hook Tavern, he turns his attention to a knockout burger prepared with American cheese, white onion, and wedge fries, served in a dining room made to feel like it's been there for decades. There's also fish and chips, mussels with nduja sausage, and a wedge salad with a fab slab of bacon.

24. Syko
126 Windsor Place,
Park Slope

This may be one of the only, if not *the* only, Korean Syrian restaurants in NYC. Syko combines the owner couple's respective heritages in a menu that isn't fusion so much as Korean *and* Syrian food, with dishes like chicken shawarma and something called a "Fatboy," a very messy but incredibly delicious meal where bulgogi meat is wrapped burrito-style. This take-out counter has virtually no seating, but thankfully Prospect Park is just a block or so away. Syko also makes for a great pre-movie snack before a screening at nearby Nitehawk Cinema.

25. Tacos El Bronco
860 5th Avenue,
Sunset Park

There are two locations of Tacos El Bronco in Sunset Park: a food truck and a sit-down restaurant. The food, for whatever reason, is always better at its taco cart. Located conveniently down the street from Melody Lanes bowling alley, this is a fun late-night option, if you don't mind balancing a paper plate with tacos on your knee while seated on a street ledge. Bring cash.

26. Tatiana
3152 Brighton 6th Street,
Brighton Beach

"Dinner and a show" takes on a new meaning at Brighton Beach's Tatiana, where the entertainment is admittedly better than the food. Watch flamethrowers and sword tricks while dining on eastern European delights like Georgian khachapuri, vareniki (Russian dumplings) served with sour cherries, and ice-cold vodka. You can order à la carte or do a set menu (better for big groups). It's all located on the boardwalk, just steps from the sand, but Tatiana is a great wintertime pick, too.

27. Ugly Baby
407 Smith Street,
Carroll Gardens

From the outside, Ugly Baby is easy to miss, located on a residential street facing the elevated G train. But this Thai favorite is serving up some of the spiciest—and most unforgettable—bites in Brooklyn. Menus change often, but expect more than just the typical hits like pad Thai. The laab ped udon, a duck salad dish, is a must-try, but be warned it's considered one of Ugly Baby's spiciest.

28. Ursula
387A Nostrand Avenue,
Bed-Stuy

Formerly a counter-service restaurant in Crown Heights that drew lines down the block for its breakfast burritos, Ursula now has bigger digs in Bed-Stuy, with room to hang out throughout the day. Eric See, a native of New Mexico, showcases the Land of Enchantment's signature green Hatch chiles that give his oozy, pressed, egg-laden burritos some spice and color. Other New Mexican specialties, like sopaipillas, are also available here.

29. Winner

367 7th Avenue,
Park Slope

Daniel Eddy's bakery brought a ton of buzz to Park Slope when it opened in 2020. The excitement hasn't waned since, so you'll want to go early to grab the donuts, croissants, and loaves of bread that have made it an essential breakfast pick, a couple of blocks away from the park. Winner now has a next-door wine bar, a Crown Heights sandwich shop and bar, a butcher shop in Park Slope, and an additional location in Prospect Park's Picnic House.

30. Yemen Café

176 Atlantic Avenue,
Cobble Hill

Atlantic Avenue in Cobble Hill is teeming with Middle Eastern bakeries and grocery stores like Sahadi's (page 161) and Damascus, and it's here you'll find Yemen Café (which also has outposts in Bay Ridge and Staten Island). Open since 1986, Yemen Café claims to be America's first Yemeni restaurant. Find halal-friendly options like foul, the tomato-based fava bean dish; root vegetable stew chicken saltah; and the lamb broth soup called marag.

QR CODES for our online guides to **BROOKLYN** neighborhoods:

BAY RIDGE

BED-STUY

CROWN HEIGHTS

DUMBO

FORT GREENE/
CLINTON HILL

PROSPECT
HEIGHTS

RED HOOK

SUNSET PARK

THE REST OF BROOKLYN
SHOPPING

Brooklyn would be the third-biggest city in the United States if it were a city, as it was until 1898. And traveling through this part of the borough, even setting the neighborhoods in North Brooklyn aside, you'll encounter all the diversity of a major metropolis. There are the picturesque streets of brownstone Brooklyn, a designation that exists in the popular imagination and in multiple actual neighborhoods in this borough; the Caribbean communities south of Prospect Park; the enduring Italian American roots of Carroll Gardens. And while there may be few descriptions that could apply to all of these neighborhoods, an overall food scene as vibrant as you'll find in Manhattan means that there's plenty to seek out for those who appreciate eating, cooking, and entertaining.

1. Brooklyn Flea
80 Pearl Street,
Dumbo
Unlike the associated Smorgasburg, where you'll encounter vendors serving all the food you could want to eat, if not food to take home with you, Brooklyn Flea is not on its face a food destination. But it is a shopping destination, and among the vendors in the shadow of the Brooklyn Bridge, you'll find antique and vintage kitchenware and other home goods, plus a rotating cohort of artisans selling their creations, edibles like herbal tea blends and small-batch spices included. An indoor version of the market is open year-round in Chelsea, but for the Brooklyn original, visit on weekend days in April through December.

2. Fermented Grapes
651 Vanderbilt Avenue,
Prospect Heights
Although this Prospect Heights shop has been around for some time, since new owner Kilolo Strobert took over Fermented Grapes with business partner Max Katzenberg in 2021, it's become more than your average neighborhood wine store. Strobert, a Brooklynite who was the shop's first full-time employee, stocks natural and biodynamic wines, dedicating sections to female, Black, and Indigenous

winemakers, plus spirits from both small, local producers and the bigger guys. But more than any one category of drink, a welcoming ethos is the priority.

3. Grand Army Plaza Greenmarket
Grand Army Plaza,
Prospect Heights
While not quite as large as its Union Square counterpart, the Saturday greenmarket at Grand Army Plaza is Brooklyn's flagship farmers' market. You can expect the usual mix of produce, flowers, baked goods, and maple syrup from upstate. Given its location, right at the northernmost entrance to leafy Prospect Park and just blocks away from the Brooklyn Museum and Brooklyn Botanic Garden, it's a fantastic place to kick off a Saturday in Brooklyn.

4. Jacques Torres
66 Water Street,
Dumbo
Jacques Torres is a storied name in chocolate for good reason. And it only makes sense that his original location is in Dumbo, arguably (and understandably) Brooklyn's most recognizable neighborhood. After joining the crowds to snap photos of the Brooklyn Bridge at the intersection of Washington and Water Streets, walk two minutes to shop handmade truffles, bars, holiday-themed

treats, and tins of the best hot chocolate around. Depending on the season, you'll also want to order up a cup of hot chocolate, an ice cream sandwich, or perhaps some chocolate chip cookies to enjoy as you wander Dumbo's picturesque streets.

5. Japan Village at Industry City
934 3rd Avenue,
Sunset Park
The sixteen-building developer complex known as Industry City houses artists' studios, office space, food halls, and destination-worthy shopping for vintage fashions, furniture, and, of course, food. To satisfy that last point, start at Japan Village in Building 3. Next to a food court serving udon, taiyaki, and other Japanese fare, there's a spacious—for—New York outpost of Sunrise Mart, the Japanese grocery store. Nearby, bottle shop Kuraichi sells Japanese spirits and sake. For other food shopping, note that Industry City is also home to a second outpost of Sahadi's (page 161), with an attached restaurant.

6. Kings County Distillery
299 Sands Street,
Brooklyn Navy Yard
At Kings County Distillery, you can pick up some pints of locally made whiskey while visiting a piece of Brooklyn history. The tasting

8. Marché Rue Dix
1453 Bedford Avenue,
Crown Heights

At the concept store next to Crown Heights French-Senegalese restaurant Cafe Rue Dix, the Rue Dix brand sells its own line of clothes, accessories, and home goods. The latter category includes some of the same hot sauce, spices, tea, and coffee you'll see on the restaurant's menu, all in highly giftable black-and-gold packaging.

9. Mazzola Bakery
192 Union Street,
Carroll Gardens

It's difficult to select just one Italian bakery to shop in Carroll Gardens, a historically Italian Brooklyn neighborhood. But Mazzola is a clear standout. The lard bread is the stuff of neigh-borhood legend (and makes an excellent host gift). And although they're not talked about nearly as much, the rainbow cookies are some of the best in the city. If you visit around Christmastime, note the Mazzola tradition of hoisting a full-sized Christmas tree onto the front of the building as you pick up gift boxes full of Italian cookies priced by the pound.

room and shop are located inside the gatehouses, the medieval castle–like structure that formed the entrance to the Brooklyn Navy Yard, a once-active naval shipyard first opened in 1801. And although a food court that includes an outpost of Russ & Daughters (page 44) has since opened up, when Kings County Distillery set up shop in 2012, it became one of the first businesses to draw the public out to the quiet industrial complex. It's since built a reputation for award-winning bourbons and moonshines, all distilled in Brooklyn. That distillery, just beyond the tasting room, is also open for tours.

7. Labay Market
1127 Nostrand Avenue,
Prospect Lefferts Gardens

In Prospect Lefferts Gardens, one of a few neighborhoods in this part of Brooklyn that are home to a large West Indian community, Labay Market is a hub for all the tastes of home. Soursop, sorrel, sea moss, and other hard-to-find produce are available here, sourced from the owner's sixty-acre Grenada farm. The Grenada con-nection means you'll also find Grenadian chocolates and island spices such as nutmeg and cinnamon. The customer service gets con-sistently positive reviews.

10. Sahadi's

187 Atlantic Avenue,
Brooklyn Heights

Sahadi's has been a destination grocery store since the 1940s, as one of the cluster of Middle Eastern businesses on this stretch of Atlantic; it was named a James Beard America's Classic in 2017. At the entrance, grab a ticket to shop bulk dry goods from glass jars, including figs, apricots, nuts, and coffee, then at the deli counter just beyond, order containers of hummus and labneh, bourekas, and baklava—and take the entire haul over to Brooklyn Bridge Park for a picnic.

11. Salter House

119 Atlantic Avenue,
Brooklyn Heights

At Salter House, Sandeep Salter has assembled a range of household goods that all speak to her particular vision for domestic life, one that's perhaps best described as countryside chic by way of Brooklyn. In practice, this means scallop-edged porcelain, enamelware pots, sustainable table linens, and cleaning supplies that double as decorative objects.

Brooklynites also flock to the shop for its collection of floral corsets and feminine sleepwear. Adding to the charm: an in-store café selling coffee and tea and vegan baked goods.

12. Whisk

197 Atlantic Avenue,
Brooklyn Heights

Just down the block from Sahadi's, Whisk is the go-to kitchenware store for Brooklyn home cooks. Although you'll find all the practical tools you could need to supply a cooking hobby, the inviting shop also offers plenty to look at, with cutesy mugs, linens, and totes stocked among the skillets and meat thermometers.

BEYOND RESTAURANTS

Coffee Shops
% Arabica
Corto
Villager
Yafa Cafe

Bars
Clover Club
Grand Army
Leyenda
Sunken Harbor Club

Bakeries
Agi's Counter
ByClio Bakery
Fan-Fan Doughnuts
L'Appartement 4F
Otway Bakery

Ice Cream
Brooklyn Farmacy and
    Soda Fountain
Malai Ice Cream
OddFellows
The Social
Sweet Dynasty Ice
    Cream

HOW TO GET A SEAT AT THE TABLE:

From reservations to walk-ins

By Emma Orlow

Getting a reservation in New York City is notoriously difficult, verging on masochistic. But thankfully, over the years covering New York's dining scene, we've gathered some tips for how to make the most of your time dining out in New York.

Plan ahead

Resy is the most-used booking platform for hot new restaurants—and increasingly bars—in New York City. Ideally, start making your dining wish list more than one month in advance, as many places allow you to make reservations four weeks out, although this varies considerably. If the restaurant or bar doesn't list what time their books open, call and ask in advance. Then mark your calendar and be sure to set a reminder. If the reservation window opens at ten A.M., log in exactly at that time to try to avoid being disappointed. However, if your ideal spot is already booked, there are a few things you can still do . . .

Get on the wait list

Add yourself to the wait list in OpenTable, Resy, or Tock, if available, and turn on your notifications so you are the first to see when a table opens up that fits your parameters. New Yorkers are planners, but they can also be flaky—especially if there's bad weather that night. Often a restaurant has more reservations available than what's put into the apps. It's worth emailing or calling the restaurant directly to see if they can squeeze you in.

Walk in

Likewise, plenty of restaurants leave space for walk-ins (you can even ask them what percentage of the restaurant they leave for walk-ins to better gauge your chances). If you don't have a reservation, you'll have the most luck as a walk-in going alone—sitting at the bar is the easiest spot

in a restaurant to get. If you want to stop by with a group, just make sure you're picking a restaurant that didn't just open, and therefore isn't going to have the hype machine drumming up crowds. As always, the best time to hit a restaurant without a reservation is going when the spot first opens, and either eating with the early birds or putting your name down for later, and getting a drink to fill up the hours-long wait. Or try later in the evening, past the prime-time rush.

Try no-reservation spots

Plenty of restaurants don't take reservations, thus leveling the playing field for those of us who forgot to or don't like to plan ahead. Bernie's (page 129) in Greenpoint, the Fly in Clinton Hill, Astoria Seafood (page 105) in Queens, Kiki's (page 37) on the Lower East Side, and Hop Lee in Chinatown are just a few.

Mostly, just be flexible and have an open mind. Try a place that was buzzy five years ago instead of right this moment. And if you don't get into your hit list place, there are thousands of other wonderful and surprising places you can try.

HOTELS WITH THE BEST FOOD BUILT IN

As You Are at Ace Hotel Brooklyn
252 Schermerhorn Street,
Downtown Brooklyn, Brooklyn
The Downtown Brooklyn location of the Ace is a great option if you're trying to bop around: not too far from shopping in Carroll Gardens, Prospect Park, or the strip of heavy-hitter restaurants in Prospect Heights. But the hotel itself is a vibe: A sexy hotel bar is a great meeting spot, and As You Are, the lobby restaurant, can stand on its own. After a half decade away from the New York restaurant scene, Camille Becerra, a *Top Chef* alum, returned to the hotel, giving its menu an update that pulls from her Puerto Rican roots mixed with notes reminiscent of modern wellness culture.

Burger Joint at the Thompson Central Park
119 West 56th Street,
Midtown West, Manhattan
Yes, you can pretend to be Eloise and stay at the Plaza, or you can stay just a short walk away at the less-coveted Thompson Central Park, also overlooking the city's largest green space. The real reason to come here over the views is Burger Joint (page 69), a burger spot made to look like a dive bar of sorts, which has one of NYC's best burgers. Burger Joint is often referred to as a speakeasy—it's hidden behind a curtain—but it's fair to say the secret is out on this one.

Corner Bar at Nine Orchard
60 Canal Street, Lower East Side, Manhattan
Nine Orchard's food is handled by Ignacio Mattos of Estela (page 36) fame. Corner Bar offers a great weekday breakfast and weekend brunch, while the Swan Room is a luxe spot for a pre-dinner cocktail or a nightcap before heading up to your room.

Dowling's at the Carlyle
35 East 76th Street,
Upper East Side, Manhattan
The Carlyle, first opened a century ago in 1930, is Upper East Side luxury at its apex. This iconic hotel is most known for its bar Bemelmans, a posh hang with murals by the creator of the *Madeline* book series. Lesser known is the property's equally luxe Dowling's, which opened in 2021, in a kitchen led by a former 21 Club chef. Focused on mid-nineteenth-century nostalgia, the menu features classic Americana dishes like steak Diane in a room with walls covered with paintings.

Laser Wolf at the Hoxton
97 Wythe Avenue, Williamsburg, Brooklyn
The esteemed Michael Solomonov is the chef behind Philly's hottest restaurants. But you don't have to go to Philly to check out Laser Wolf, an outpost of his Israeli grill house at the Williamsburg Hoxton hotel. The draws here include the incredible views of the Manhattan skyline and the dips that come complimentary with each meal, like hummus, baba ghanoush, Turkish celery root, and mushrooms with chard and sour cherry. Downstairs, Solomonov opened a NYC outpost of K'Far, and though dinner is available here, too, brunch is more popular, with its

Jerusalem bagel egg sandwiches and sticky pistachio buns.

Le Coucou at 11 Howard

138 Lafayette Street, Little Italy, Manhattan

Le Coucou, the acclaimed, Michelin-starred French restaurant from Stephen Starr and chef Daniel Rose, is located in the heart of downtown Manhattan. For a taste of New York fine dining, this restaurant is a splurge that does it right.

Le Crocodile at the Wythe Hotel

80 Wythe Avenue, Williamsburg, Brooklyn

From the team behind brunch favorite Chez Ma Tante, Le Crocodile (page 131) is a brasserie located in the Wythe Hotel with tall ceilings and romantic lighting perfect for an impressive date night. The move here is the roast chicken and one of the many desserts. Head upstairs after for a drink at Bar Blondeau, a rooftop bar with bites that can back up the views.

Soho Diner at the Soho Grand

320 West Broadway, Soho, Manhattan

When it comes to breakfast for dinner, a diner is the way to go. But diners are becoming harder and harder to come by in New York City. This newfangled spot located in the Soho Grand brings the same nostalgic feeling with an updated menu: think buttermilk pancakes with preserved lemon, kale Caesar salad, matzo ball soup, and a fun line of cocktails like an orange Julius, espresso martinis, and orange wine.

Zaytinya at the Ritz-Carlton

1185 Broadway, Nomad, Manhattan

Celebrity chef José Andrés brought his acclaimed Eastern Mediterranean Zaytinya—a staple in DC for two decades—to the Ritz-Carlton in Nomad. Smaller and more intimate than its DC counterpart, a favorite among political bigwigs, the dining room was designed by the Rockwell Group, behind some of NYC's most major restaurants, with a menu that looks to Greece, Turkey, and Lebanon for its point of view.

WHERE TO EAT NEAR MAJOR TOURIST ATTRACTIONS

American Museum of Natural History
▶ Jing Fong UWS (page 87)
380 Amsterdam Avenue, Upper West Side, Manhattan

Apollo Theater
▶ Red Rooster (page 88)
310 Lenox Avenue, Harlem, Manhattan

Brighton Beach
▶ Kashkar Cafe (page 154)
1141 Brighton Beach Avenue, Brighton Beach, Brooklyn

Bronx Zoo
▶ Zero Otto Nove (page 99)
2357 Arthur Avenue, Belmont, Bronx

Brooklyn Bridge
▶ Celestine
1 John Street, Dumbo, Brooklyn

Brooklyn Museum
▶ Agi's Counter
818 Franklin Avenue, Crown Heights, Brooklyn

Central Park
▶ Mission Ceviche (page 87)
1400 2nd Avenue, Upper East Side, Manhattan

Chinatown
▶ Nom Wah Tea Parlor (page 37)
13 Doyers Street, Chinatown, Manhattan

▶ Uncle Lou (page 39)
73 Mulberry Street, Chinatown, Manhattan

Citi Field
▶ Chongqing Lao Zao
37-04 Prince Street, Flushing, Queens

Coney Island
▶ Totonno's (page 51)
1524 Neptune Avenue, Coney Island, Brooklyn

Empire State Building
▶ Let's Meat BBQ
307 5th Avenue, Koreatown, Manhattan

Grand Central
▶ Grand Central Oyster Bar (page 70)
89 East 42nd Street (Grand Central Terminal), Midtown East, Manhattan

High Line
▶ Chama Mama
149 West 14th Street, Chelsea, Manhattan

▶ Los Tacos No. 1 at Chelsea Market (page 14)
75 9th Avenue, Chelsea, Manhattan

Kings Theatre
▶ Purple Yam (page 158)
1314 Cortelyou Road, Flatbush, Brooklyn

Lincoln Center
▶ Cafe Luxembourg
200 West 70th Street, Upper West Side, Manhattan

▶ P.J. Clarke's (page 72)
44 West 63rd Street, Lincoln Square, Manhattan

Metropolitan Museum of Art
► Café Sabarsky
1048 5th Avenue, Upper East Side, Manhattan

MoMA PS1
► Sami's Kabab House (page 108)
47-38 Vernon Boulevard, Astoria, Queens

Museum of the City of New York/ El Museo del Barrio
► El Tepeyac Food Market
1621 A Lexington Avenue,
East Harlem, Manhattan

► Teranga (page 89)
1280 5th Avenue, East Harlem, Manhattan

New Museum
► Cocoron (page 36)
16 Delancey Street,
Lower East Side, Manhattan

Penn Station
► Cho Dang Gol
55 West 35th Street, Koreatown, Manhattan

Prospect Park
► Fausto
348 Flatbush Avenue, Park Slope, Brooklyn

► Syko (page 156)
126 Windsor Place, Park Slope, Brooklyn

Rockefeller Center
► Le Rock (page 71)
45 Rockefeller Plaza, Rockefeller Center,
Manhattan

South Street Seaport
► The Tin Building (page 39)
96 South Street, Financial District, Manhattan

Staten Island Ferry
► Lakruwana (page 63)
668 Bay Street,
Stapleton Heights, Staten Island

► New Asha
322 Victory Boulevard,
Tompkinsville, Staten Island

Tenement Museum
► Scarr's Pizza (page 38)
35 Orchard Street,
Lower East Side, Manhattan

Times Square/Broadway
► Donburiya (page 69)
253 West 55th Street,
Hell's Kitchen, Manhattan

► Pio Pio 8
604 10th Avenue, Hell's Kitchen, Manhattan

Wall Street
► Crown Shy
70 Pine Street, Financial District, Manhattan

Washington Square Park
► Mamoun's Falafel (page 14)
119 MacDougal Street,
Greenwich Village, Manhattan

Yankee Stadium
► Papaye (page 98)
196 McClellan Street,
Concourse Village, Bronx

ACKNOWLEDGMENTS

Thank you to the Eater team behind this book, who took their love of the New York food scene and painstakingly turned it into a smart, delightful guide to the city—particularly Emma Orlow and Monica Burton, who authored the restaurant and shopping listings. Thank you to Britt Aboutaleb and Amanda Kludt for bringing this idea to life, to Ellie Krupnick and Lesley Suter for keeping us all on track, to Nat Belkov for the design collaboration, to Justine Jones for fact-checking, and to Stephanie Wu for being the guiding force. Thank you to Vox Media's Eric Karp and Hilary Sharp for literally making the deal happen, and to Aude White and Dane McMillan for making sure people know about it.

Thank you to Laura Dozier and Diane Shaw at Abrams for teaching all of us how to make a guidebook! And for their patience on a project with so many cooks. Thank you to Natasha Martin, Mamie Sanders, and Danielle Kolodkin at Abrams for their enthusiastic publicity and marketing efforts.

And most important, thank you to the sensational writers, editors, reporters, illustrators, and designers who have contributed to Eater New York over the past fifteen-plus years; this book would not have been possible without your passion and your enduring work.

CONTRIBUTORS

Erika Adams is the editor of Eater Boston. She was previously the deputy editor for Eater NY, helping to oversee service, news, and restaurant review coverage. Her writing has been published in a variety of media outlets, including *Food & Wine*, *New York*, Atlas Obscura, and the Business of Fashion.

Monica Burton is the deputy editor at Eater.com, where she also helms the site's shopping coverage, including writing Eater's weekly shopping-focused newsletter, Add to Cart. She lives in Brooklyn, New York.

Luke Fortney has been a reporter with Eater NY since 2020. He covers food trends in New York City and has written about late-night dining, reservation scalpers, and other ways the pandemic has changed the way we eat. He lives in Brooklyn, New York.

Emma Orlow is a reporter for Eater NY covering restaurants, bars, pop-ups, and the people powering them. She was born and raised in New York City and has freelanced for the *New York Times*, Grub Street, *Bon Appétit*, the *Los Angeles Times*, and more. She loves vintage 1970s cookbooks, Jell-O, and good ol'-fashioned tuna melts.

Jaya Saxena is a correspondent at Eater.com. Previously, she's written for *GQ*, *Elle*, the *Atlantic*, the *Village Voice*, Gothamist, and more. She lives in Queens, New York.

Robert Sietsema grew up in Illinois, Michigan, and Texas before moving to New York City after college. He worked as a photo editor, secretary, and rock musician before becoming a food writer. In that capacity he wrote for the *Village Voice*, *Gourmet*, and the *New York Times* before becoming Eater NY's senior critic in 2014.

Ryan Sutton is a Hell's Kitchen–based writer and journalism professor. He was the chief restaurant critic at Eater NY from 2014 until 2023; he was also a longtime food critic at Bloomberg News. Ryan writes extensively about labor issues in the hospitality industry, and he teaches "Writing Critically About Food and Restaurants" at CUNY's Craig Newmark Graduate School of Journalism. You can often find him cycling around the city, in search of a good pastry.

INDEX

Page references in *italics* refer to illustrations.

A

A&A Bake and Doubles, *150–51*, 153
ABC Kitchen, 52
Ace Hotel Brooklyn, 164
Achilles Heel, *126–27*, 129
Africa Kine, *82–83*, 85
Agi's Counter, 161, 166
Aigner Chocolates, *102–3*, 111
Al Badawi, *150–51*, 153
Alphabet City, Manhattan, 29, *32–33*, 35, 37, 38, 44, 115
Altro Paradiso, *8–9*, 12
The Amsterdam, 144
Anable Basin Sailing, 121
appetizing stores, 44, 77, 85, 90, *126–27*, 131
Aquavit, 62, *66–67*, 69
Archestratus Books + Foods, *126–27*, 135
Arepa Lady, *102–3*, 105, 114
Arthur Avenue Retail Market, 99
Arzu Palace, 55–56
Astoria, Queens, *102–3*, 104, 105, 108–9, 110, 111–12, 120–21, 167
As You Are, 164
Atlas Kitchen, *82–83*, 85
Atoboy, 53–54, 69
Atomix, 53–54, *66–67*, 69
Austrian food, 71, 99, 111, 146
Automat, 23
Ayada, *102–3*, 105
Ayat Staten Island, 63

B

bagels, *82–83*, 85, 86, 131, 141–42
Balthazar, 13–14, *32–33*, 35
Bamonte's, *126–27*, 129
Bánh, *82–83*, 85
Banh Mi Saigon, *32–33*, 35
Barbuto, *8–9*, 12
Barney Greengrass, 77, *82–83*, 85
Beall & Bell, 139
Beam, *126–27*, 135
Bed-Stuy, Brooklyn, 35, 49–50, 93, 96, *150–51*, 152–57
Bellocq, *126–27*, 135
Le Bernardin, 62, *66–67*, 71
Bernie's, *126–27*, 129, 163
B&H Dairy, *32–33*, 35
Big aLICe Brewing, 119
Big Night, *126–27*, 135
Birds of a Feather, *126–27*, 129
Birria-Landia, 28, *102–3*, 105
Bobwhite Counter, *32–33*, 35
bodegas, 26–27, 77, 92–97, 133, 139–40
La Boîte, *66–67*, 76
Bolivian Llama Party, *102–3*, 105
Bombay Frankie Roti Roll, *82–83*, 85
Bonnie's, *126–27*, 129
Bonnie Slotnick Cookbooks, *32–33*, 42
bookstores, *32–33*, 34, 42, 82–83, 91, *126–27*, 128, 135
Borgatti's Ravioli and Egg Noodles, 99
Bread and Salt, 49
Breads Bakery, 76, 113
breakfast/brunch, 12, 14, 15, 35, 36, 37, 38, 40, 44, 71, 73, 79, 106, 118, 131, 132, 139, 144, 145–47, 155, 164, 165
Brighton Beach, Brooklyn, 55–56, 118, 119, *150–51*, 152, 154, 156, 166
Brighton Tandir, 55–56
British/English food, 13, 19
Bronx, 98–99, 166–67
Brooklyn, 21, *150–51*, *150–51*. 152–157, 158–61. *See also* North Brooklyn; *specific neighborhoods*
Brooklyn Flea, 123, *150–51*, 159

Brooklyn Heights, *150–51*, 152, 153, 161
Bryant Park, Manhattan, 122
Bubby's, 146
Bunna Cafe, *126–27*, 130
Burger Joint, *66–67*, 69, 164
Bushwick, Brooklyn, 27, 29, 48, *126–27*, 128, 131, 132–33, 136
Buvette, 16, 146

C

Café China, *66–67*, 69
Cafe Luxembourg, 166
Cafe Mio, 144
Cafe Mogador, *32–33*, 35
Café Sabarsky, 167
Calabria Pork Store, 99
Caleta 111 Cevicheria, *102–3*, 105–6
Calle 191 Pescaderia, *82–83*, 86
Carbone, *8–9*, 12, 62
Caribbean food, 37, 46, 50, 58, 86–87, 117, 123, 153–55, 158
The Carlyle, 164
Carne Mare, 59
Carroll Gardens, Brooklyn, 47–48, *150–51*, 152, 153, 156, 155, 158, 160, 164
Casa Adela, *32–33*, 35
Casa Enrique, *102–3*, 106
El Castillo de Jagua, *32–33*, 36
Celestine, 166
Central Asian, 55–56
Central Park, 24, 68, 84, 87, 89–90, 120, 164, 166
Cervo's, *32–33*, 35–36, 78, 154
Chama Mama, 166
Chambers Street Wines, *8–9*, 18
Charles Pan-Fried Chicken, *82–83*, 86
Charlie Bird, *8–9*, 12
Cheburechnaya, 56
cheesecake, New York-style, 79, 115–16
cheese shops, *8–9*, 18, 42, 44, 75, 91, 99, 113, 115, 136
Chelsea, Manhattan, *8–9*, 10–16, 17–18, 28, 43, 57, 159, 166
Chez Ma Tante, 131, 146, 165
Chinatown, Flushing, 107–10, 111, 113–14

Chinatown, Manhattan, 21, 25–26, 28, 32, 33, 34, 36–40, 41, 45, 78–79, 87, 146, 163, 166
Chinese food, 25, 26, 34, 38, 39, 69, 52, 72, 85, 87, 106, 107, 111, 113, 129, 152, 153
Cho Dang Gol, 167
Chongqing Lao Zao, 166
chopped cheese, 26, 78, 93, 97
Chuan Tian Xia, *150–51*, 153
Ciao Ciao Disco, 117
Clinton St. Baking Company, 146
Cobble Hill, Brooklyn, 29, *150–51*, 152, 154, 157
Cocoron, *32–33*, 36, 167
Coming Soon, *32–33*, 42
The Commodore, 117, *126–27*, 130
Condo at the Surf Club, Montauk, 141
Coney Island, Brooklyn, 24, 51, 55, 118, 119, *150–51*, 152, 155, 166
Cookshop, *8–9*, 12
Coppelia, 28
Corner Bar, 60, 164
Corner Bistro, *8–9*, 12
Corner Slice, 49–50
Corona, Queens, *102–3*, 106–7
Corona Plaza, *102–3*, 106
Cote, 53, 57, 60, *66–67*, 69
Le Coucou, 62, 165
Court Square Diner, 28
Court Street Grocers, 72, *150–51*, 153
Le Crocodile, *126–27*, 131, 165
Crown Heights, Brooklyn, 86, 123, *150–51*, 152, 154, 157, 160, 166
Crown Shy, 167
Cuban food, 28, 58, 72–73
Cuts & Slices, 50

D

Dame, *8–9*, 13
Davelle, 146
Defonte's, *150–51*, 153
Delmonico's, 22–23
Denino's, 63
Despaña, *32–33*, 42
Dhamaka, 15, 26, *32–33*, 36, 115
Di An Di, *126–27*, 130
Di Fara Pizza, *150–51*, 153

Dimes Square, Manhattan, 35–36, 42, 78
dim sum, 28, 34, 37, 40, 79, 87, 104, 113
Diner, *126–27*, 128, 130, 132
Di Palo's Fine Foods, *32–33*, 42
Dominican food, 36, 86–87, 93, 97–98, 128
Donburiya, *66–67*, 69, 167
Don Pepe Tortas y Jugos, 119
The Donut Pub, 28
Dowling's, 164
Downing, Thomas, 22
Downing's Oyster House, 22
Downtown Brooklyn, 24, *150–51*, 153, 164
Downtown East, *32–33*, 34–40, 41–45
Downtown West, 5, *8–9*, 10–16, 17–20
Dumbo, Brooklyn, *150–51*, 152, 157, 159, 166
Dutch Kills, 112, 121

E

Ear Inn, *8–9*, 13
Earth & Me, *102–3*, 111
East Harlem, Manhattan, 24, 51, 67, 78, 79, *82–83*, 167
East Village, Manhattan, 26, 34–35, 36, 37, 39–43, 44, 50, 62, 74, 95, 108, 115, 133, 146
Economy Candy, *32–33*, 43
Eddie's Sweet Shop, *102–3*, 106
Edy's Grocer, *126–27*, 135
egg cream, 72, 78, 87, 115
Egger's Ice Cream Parlor, 63
Ejen, 119
Eleven Madison Park, 62, *66–67*, 69, 72, 94
Elmhurst, Queens, *102–3*, 104–6, 108
Emmett's on Grove, 51
Emmy Squared, 51–52
Empanada Mama, 28, 57–58, *66–67*, 69–70
Essex Market and Market Line, *32–33*, 36, 43, 115
Estela, 12, 60, *32–33*, 36, 164
Evelia's Tamales, *102–3*, 106

F

Factory Tamal, *32–33*, 36
Falansai, *126–27*, 130
farm-to-table, 12, 45, 130, 155
Fausto, 167
Fauzia's Heavenly Delights, 98
Fermented Grapes, *150–51*, 159
F&F Pizzeria, 47–48
Financial District, Manhattan, *32–33*, 39, 59, 62, 167
Fine & Raw Chocolate, *126–27*, 136
Fini Pizza, 47–48
Fishs Eddy, *66–67*, 75
Flagship Brewing Co., 63
Flatbush, Brooklyn, *150–51*, 155, 156, 166
Flatiron, Manhattan, 53, 54, 62, *66–67*, 68, 69, 72–73, 75, 99. *See also* Midtown and Flatiron
Flushing, Queens, 26, 56, 79, *102–3*, 104, 106, 107–10, 111–14, 166
food halls/courts, 28, 36, 39, 43, 76, 107, 111, 112, 114, 147, 159, 160
Forest Hills, Queens, 55, *102–3*, 106, 111
Fort George, Manhattan, *82–83*, 86
Fort Greene, Brooklyn, *150–51*, 155, 157
Foster Sundry, *126–27*, 136
The Four Horsemen, *126–27*, 130
Frankel's Delicatessen & Appetizing, *126–27*, 131
Frenchette, *8–9*, 13, 71

G

Gage & Tollner, *150–51*, 153–54
Gallaghers Steakhouse, 57–59,
 66–67, 70
Girasol Bakery, 28–29
Gloria's, *150–51*, 154
Goldberg's Bagels, 141–42
Golden Diner, *32–33*, 36, 146
Gosman's Gourmet Fish Market,
 142
Gowanus, Brooklyn, 21, *150–51*,
 154
Gramercy Tavern, 62, 108
Grand Army Plaza Greenmarket,
 150–51, 159
Grand Central Market, *66–67*, 75
Grand Central Oyster Bar, *66–67*,
 70, 166
Gravesend, Brooklyn, *150–51*, 154
Gray's Papaya, 24, *82–83*, 86
Greek food, 15, 24, 37, 104, 108,
 110, 120–21
Greenpoint, Brooklyn, 47–48, 128–
 30, 131, 132–33, 135, 146, 163
Greenpoint Fish & Lobster Co.,
 126–27, 131
Greenwich Village, Manhattan
 8–9, 10–14, 19, 24, 29, 52,
 62, 167
The Grill, 61–62
Guantanamera, 58

H

Hadramout Restaurant, 29
Haenyeo, *150–51*, 154
Haidilao, *102–3*, 106
The Halal Guys, *66–67*, 70, 78–79
The Halyard, 140
Harlem, Manhattan, 24, 51, 67, 78,
 82–83, 84–86, 88–89, 90, 91,
 93, 97, 166, 167
Harlem Chocolate Factory,
 82–83, 91
Hart's, 35, *150–51*, 154
Heatonist, *126–27*, 136
Hector's Cafe & Diner, *8–9*, 13,
 117–18
Hell's Kitchen, Manhattan, 28,
 49–50, 54, 57–58, *66–67*,
 69–70, 72–73, 76, 167
Herald Square, Manhattan,
 66–67, 69, 71
H&H Bagels, *82–83*, 86
Ho Foods, 146
Homeport, 142
Hometown Bar-B-Que, 60,
 150–51, 154, 156
Hoxton, 164
Hudson Valley, 61, 75, 143–45

I

immigrants, 23, 25–27, 34, 41, 46,
 51, 79, 87–88, 95, 99, 128, 153
Immigration and Nationality Act
 of 1965, 25
Indian food, 15, 26, 36, *66–67*, 70,
 78, 85, 106, 109, 114, 115
L'Industrie Pizzeria, 47–48
Insa, *150–51*, 154
La Isla, 29
Izzy's Smokehouse, *82–83*, 86

J

Jackson Diner, *102–3*, 106
Jackson Heights, Queens, 26, 28,
 29, 42, *102–3*, 104–9, 114
Jacob's Pickles, *82–83*, 86
Jacques Torres, *150–51*, 159
Jamaica, Queens, *102–3*, 109
Jamaican food, 27, 37, 98, 119, 155
J. B. Prince Company, *66–67*, 75
Jeffrey's Grocery, *8–9*, 14
Jersey City, New Jersey, 26, 49
JG Melon, *82–83*, 86–87
Jing Fong, *82–83*, 87, 166
Joe & Pat's, 50
Joe's Pizza, 46–47
John Derian Company Inc.,
 32–33, 43
John's of Bleecker Street, *8–9*,
 14, 24, 51
Jongro Gopchang, 60, *66–67*, 70
Joomak Banjum, 53–54
Jua, 54
Jungsik, 53–54

K

Kalustyan's, *66–67*, 75
Kang Ho Dong Baekjeong NYC,
 66–67, 71
Karczma, *126–27*, 131
Kashkar Cafe, 56, *150–51*, 154, 166
Katagiri Japanese Grocery,
 66–67, 75
Katz's Delicatessen, 24, *32–33*,
 36, 59–60, 79
Keens Steakhouse, 23, 57, 59,
 66–67, 71

Kee's Chocolates, *82–83*, 91
Kiki's, *32–33*, 37, 78, 163
Killmeyer's, 63
King, *8–9*, 14
King of Falafel & Shawarma, 120–21
Kings County Distillery, *150–51*, 159–60
Kips Bay, Manhattan, *66–67*, 69, 75
Kitchen Arts & Letters, *82–83*, 91
Kjun, *66–67*, 71
Koloman, *66–67*, 71, 146
Kopitiam, *32–33*, 37, 147
Koreatown, Manhattan, 29, 53–54, *66–67*, 68, 70–72, 166–67
Kreuther Handcrafted Chocolate, *66–67*, 76

L

Labay Market, *150–51*, 160
Lakruwana, 63, 167
Laser Wolf, 164–65
L&B Spumoni Gardens, 50, 79, *150–51*, 154
Lee's Tavern, 63
The Lemon Ice King of Corona, *102–3*, 107
Leo, 48, *126–27*, 131
Let's Meat BBQ, 166
Leventhal, Ben, 4
Lexington Candy Shop, *82–83*, 87
Liebman's Deli, 24, 98
Lilia, *126–27*, 131
Lincoln Square, Manhattan, *82–83*, 87, 89, 166
Little India, Jackson Heights, 104, 106
Little Italy, Bronx, 90, 99
Little Italy, Manhattan, 24, *32–33*, 34–35, 40, 42, 62, 122, 165
Llama Inn, *126–27*, 131
Llama San, 62
Lockwood, *102–3*, 111
Lodi, *66–67*, 72
Lombardi's, 14, 24, 51
Long Island, 22, 46, 61, 138–43
The Long Island Bar, *150–51*, 154–55

Long Island City, Queens, 28, *102–3*, 106, 108–9, 111–12, 121
Loring Place, 52
Louie & Ernie's Pizza, 98
Lower East Side, Manhattan, 24, 28, 34–37, 38, 39, 40, 41–44, 47, 48, 115, 128, 146–47, 154, 163, 164, 167
Lucali, *150–51*, 155
Lysée, 54

M

Main Road Biscuit Co., 139
Maison Premiere, *126–27*, 132
Malaysian food, 37, 104, 146–47
Malecon, *82–83*, 87
Mamoun's Falafel, *8–9*, 14, 29, 167
Manhattan. *See* Downtown East; Downtown West; Midtown and Flatiron; Uptown; West Village; *specific neighborhoods*
Le Marais, 60–61
Marché Rue Dix, *150–51*, 160
Marea, *66–67*, 72
Margon, *66–67*, 72
Mari, 54
Marie's Crisis Café, 117
Mariscos El Submarino, *102–3*, 107
Mazzola Bakery, *150–51*, 160
McNulty's Tea & Coffee Co, *8–9*, 18
The Meadow, *32–33*, 43
The Meat Hook, *126–27*, 137
Mediterranean food, 14–15, 29, 111, 120–21, 154, 164–65
Metropolitan Museum of Art, 24, 84, 87, 120, 167
Midtown and Flatiron, 54–56, 58, 60–62, *66–67*, 68–73, 74–76, 164, 166
Midwood, Brooklyn, *150–51*, 153
The Migrant Kitchen, *82–83*, 87
Milu, *66–67*, 72
Minetta Tavern, *8–9*, 14
Misi, 116, 131
Miss Ada, *150–51*, 155
Mission Ceviche, *82–83*, 87, 166
Miss Lily's, *32–33*, 37
Mociun, *126–27*, 137

Mogmog, *102–3*, 111
MoMA Design Store, *66–67*, 76
Momofuku Noodle Bar, *32–33*, 37
Mondel Chocolates, *82–83*, 91
Murray Hill, Manhattan, 26, 62, *66–67*, 71
Murray's Cheese, *8–9*, 18, 75, 136

N

Nalata Nalata, *32–33*, 43
Nan Xiang Xiao Long Bao, *102–3*, 107, 113
Nargis Cafe, 55–56
Nathan's Famous, 24, 55, 119, *150–51*, 152, 155
Native Noodles, *82–83*, 88
Nepalese food, 26, *102–3*, 104, 107, 109, 114
New Asha, 167
New Flushing Bakery, 114
New World Mall, *102–3*, 107, 111, 114
New York. *See specific topics*
New York City Wine & Food Festival, 122
969 NYC Coffee, *102–3*, 105
Nine Orchard hotel, 12, 78, 164
Nolita, Manhattan, 34–35, 36, 37, 38, 40, 42–44, 50, 51, 147
Nomad, Manhattan, 54, *66–67*, 71, 75, 146, 165
Nom Wah Tea Parlor, *32–33*, 37, 166
North Brooklyn, 5, *126–27*, 128–33, 134–37
North Fork, Long Island, 138–40
North Fork Roasting Co., 139
Nurlan, 56
NY Cake, *8–9*, 18
NY Dosas, *8–9*, 14

O

Oasis, *126–27*, 132
The Odeon, *8–9*, 15
Oiji Mi, 53–54
Okonomi, 147
Old Homestead, 57
Olmsted, *150–51*, 155
188 Bakery Cuchifritos, 78, 98
Open Streets program, 122

Ops, 48
Orient Country Store, 139–40
Oxomoco, *126–27*, 132

P

Palestinian food, 27, 63, 120, 132, 152–53
Papaya Dog, 29
Papaye, 98, 167
Park Slope, Brooklyn, 28, 95, *150–51*, 154, 156–57, 167
Parrot Coffee, *102–3*, 111
Pastis, 14, 60
Patel Brothers, 106, 114
Patsy's, 24, 51
Paulie Gee's Slice Shop, 47–48
Peaches HotHouse, *150–51*, 155
Penn Station, 72
Peoples Wine, 43, 115
Peppa's, *150–51*, 155
Peruvian food, 62, 87, 105–6, 131
Peter Luger Steak House, 57, 116, *126–27*, 132
Peter Pan Donut & Pastry Shop, *126–27*, 132
Le Petit Bistro, 145
Phil-Am Food Mart, *102–3*, 112
The Pickle Guys, *32–33*, 43–44
Pies 'n' Thighs, *126–27*, 132
Pio Pio 8, 167
Una Pizza Napoletana, 48
P.J. Clarke's, *66–67*, 72, 166
Pocha 32, 29, *66–67*, 72
Polish food, 104, 128, 131

Porto Rico Importing Co., *8–9*, 19
Prospect Heights, Brooklyn, *150–51*, 152, 155, 157, 159
Puerto Rican food, 29, 35, 78, 98, 128, 164
Punjabi Deli, *32–33*, 37–38, 96
Pupusas Ridgewood, *102–3*, 107
Purple Yam, *150–51*, 156, 166

Q

Queens, 21, 55, *102–3*, 104–9, 110–12, 122. *See also specific neighborhoods*
El Quijote, *8–9*, 13

R

Raoul's, *8–9*, 15, 60
Ray's Candy Store, 115
Razza, 49
Red Hook, Brooklyn, *150–51*, 153–54, 156–57
Red Rooster, *82–83*, 88, 166
Reggae Town Cafe, 119
Rego Park, Queens, 55–56, *102–3*
Restaurant Week, 123
Richmond Hill, Queens, *102–3*, 105–6
Ridgewood, Queens, *102–3*, 104, 107–9, 111
Rio Market, *102–3*, 112
Ritz-Carlton, 165
Roberta's, 48, *126–27*, 132
Roberto's, 98
Le Rock, *66–67*, 71, 167
Rocka Rolla, 117
Rockaway Beach, Queens, *102–3*, 108
Rockefeller Center, Manhattan, 14, *66–67*, 68, 71–72, 155, 167
Rolo's, *102–3*, 108
Roman and Williams Guild, *8–9*, 19
Rubirosa, 50
Russ & Daughters, *32–33*, 44, 77, 160
Russo's, 115
Ruta Oaxaca, *102–3*, 108

S

Saga, 62
Sahadi's, *150–51*, 159, 161
Salter House, *150–51*, 161
Salvadoran food, 27, 107
Sami's Kabab House, *102–3*, 108, 167
Sandwich and Pickle, 63
Santa Ana Deli & Grocery, *126–27*, 133
Scarr's Pizza, *32–33*, 38, 47, 167
Schaller & Weber, *82–83*, 88
2nd Ave Deli, 59, *82–83*, 85
Semma, *8–9*, 15
Sheepshead Bay, Brooklyn, 55–56, *150–51*
Sherdor, 55–56
Shu Jiao Fu Zhou, *32–33*, 38
Shukette, *8–9*, 15
Shuko, 62
668 the Gig Shack, 143
Slovak-Czech Varieties, *102–3*, 112
Smith & Wollensky, 58
Smorgasburg, 123, 159
Soho, Manhattan, *8–9*, 10–14, 15, 16, 17, 19, 42, 76, 165
SOS Chefs, *32–33*, 44
Sound View Greenport, 138–39
South Edison, 143
South Indian food, 14–15, 108–9
Southold General, 139
Spanish food, 13, 16, 27, 35–36, 42, 147
Spicy Village, *32–33*, 38
S&P Lunch, *66–67*, 72
splurges, 15, 52, 62, 165
Sri Lankan food, 26, 63
St. Anselm, *126–27*, 133
Staten Island, 50, 56, 63, 157, 167
Steele, Lockhart, 4
Stick With Me Sweets, *32–33*, 44
Stissing House, 145
street food, 22–24, 77, 79, 85, 97–98, 104, 106, 109
Sullivan Street Bakery, *8–9*, 15, 48–49
Sunny & Annie's, 29
Sunnyside, Queens, *102–3*, 105, 111
Sunset Park, Brooklyn, 119, *150–51*, 152, 153, 156–57, 159

FRESCAS

PALETAS

PALETAS

FRESCAS

Superiority Burger, 29, *32–33*, 38
Sushi Noz, *82–83*, 88
Sushi on Me, *102–3*, 108
Syko, *150–51*, 156, 167
Sylvia's, *82–83*, 84, 88

T

Taam Tov, 55–56
Tacos El Bronco, *150–51*, 156
Los Tacos No. 1 (Chelsea Market),
    8–9, 14, 18, 61, 166
Tacoway Beach, *102–3*, 108
Taïm, *8–9*, 15
Taqueria 86, *82–83*, 88
Taqueria Ramirez, *126–27*, 133
Tashkent Supermarket, 55–56,
    118–19
Tatiana, *150–51*, 156
Tatiana by Kwame Onwuachi,
    82–83, 89
Taverna Kyclades, *102–3*, 108
Tea & Sympathy, *8–9*, 19
Té Company, *8–9*, 19
Teitel Brothers, 99
Temple Canteen, *102–3*, 108–9
Tempura Matsui, 62
El Tepeyac Food Market, 167
Teranga, *82–83*, 89, 167
Thai food, *32–33*, 38, 72, 104–5,
    109, 147, 156
Thompson Central Park, 164
Three Roosters, *66–67*, 72
Times Square, Manhattan, 14,
    23–24, 26, 61, *66–67*, 68, 70,
    72–73, 74, 167
The Tin Building, *32–33*, 39, 167
Tom's Restaurant, *82–83*, 89
Tong, *102–3*, 109
Totonno's, 51, 166
Tribeca, Manhattan, *8–9*, 10–11,
    13, 15–16, 17–18, 53–54, 61, 146
Trinidadian food, 27, 78, 152–54
Txikito, *8–9*, 16

U

Ugly Baby, *150–51*, 156
Ukrainian food, 4, 27, 34, 39, 152
Uncle Lou, *32–33*, 39, 166

Union Square Greenmarket,
    32–33, 44–45, 113
Upper East Side, Manhattan,
    82–83, 85–89, 91, 164, 166–67
Upper West Side, Manhattan, 26,
    82–83, 85–89, 91, 166
Uptown, *82–83*, 85–89, 90–91
Ursula, *150–51*, 156

V

Veniero's Pasticceria & Caffe, 115
Veselka, *32–33*, 34, 39
Via Carota, *8–9*, 16
Victor's Café, *66–67*, 73

W

Washington Heights, Manhattan,
    82–83, 84, 87–88
Wenwen, *126–27*, 133
West Indian Day Parade, 123
West Village, *8–9*, 10–12, 14–16,
    17–19, 29, 46–47, 51, 62, 117,
    135, 146
While in Kathmandu, *102–3*, 109
Whisk, *150–51*, 161
White Bear, *102–3*, 109
Wildair, *32–33*, 39, 43
William Greenberg Desserts,
    82–83, 91, 120

Williamsburg, Brooklyn, 47–48,
    116–17, 123, *126–27*, 128–33,
    135–37, 147, 164–65
Wing On Wo & Co., *32–33*, 45
Winner, *150–51*, 157
Win Son, *126–27*, 133, 137, 147
Woodside, Queens, *102–3*, 110, 112
Wu's Wonton King, *32–33*, 39
Wythe Hotel, 131, 165

Y

Yakitori Torishin, *66–67*, 73
Yellow Rose, *32–33*, 40
Yemen Café, 63, *150–51*, 157
Yemeni food, 29, 63, 95, 157
Yi Ji Shi Mo, *32–33*, 40
Yun Hai Shop, *126–27*, 137
Yunhong Chopsticks, *32–33*, 45

Z

Zaab Zaab, *102–3*, 109
Zabar's, 75, 77, *82–83*, 91
Zaytinya, 165
Zero Otto Nove, 99, 166

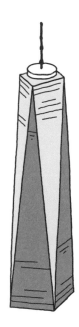

Editor: Laura Dozier
Designer: Jenice Kim
Managing Editor: Lisa Silverman
Production Manager: Larry Pekarek

Library of Congress Control Number: 2023945800

ISBN: 978-1-4197-6581-0
eISBN: 978-1-64700-889-5

Text and illustrations copyright © 2024 Vox Media, Inc.
Illustrations by Naomi Otsu

Cover © 2024 Abrams

Printed and bound in the United States
10 9 8 7 6 5 4 3 2 1

Abrams books are available at special discounts when purchased in quantity
for premiums and promotions as well as fundraising or educational use.
Special editions can also be created to specification. For details, contact
specialsales@abramsbooks.com or the address below.

Abrams Image® is a registered trademark of Harry N. Abrams, Inc.

ABRAMS The Art of Books
195 Broadway, New York, NY 10007
abramsbooks.com